Slow Down, Mama

Intentional Living
in a
Hurried World

Megan ♡
You are precious.
Thank you for
having me come
speak. God bless
you as you
slow and
savor.
♡
Patty
Ps 46:10

By Patty H. Scott, MA

COPYRIGHT

Copyright © 2018 by Patty H. Scott

Contact Patty Scott @
www.pattyhscott.com

pjpsalm103@sbcglobal.net

Cover photo credits: Joshua Reddekopp

DEDICATION

This book is dedicated to you. Can you believe it? You finally have a dedication just for you. In all seriousness, I dedicate this book to the weary and worn out woman, to the mom needing to get ahead of her to-do list, to those of us just wanting to catch a breath. May you find hope and tools here, and the inspiration to make real changes.

Introduction

I'm so glad you are here. This book grew out of my personal experience of running myself ragged and missing the mark. I thought busyness was the only choice I had. I lived believing all my activity would fill me. Instead, overstuffing my life depleted my soul. I have discovered an unsuspected truth: slowing down held the key to all my deeper longings.

I want this book to do more than encourage you. My prayer is that this book will empower you to make changes so you can live your life for what matters most to you.

This book is about time, but it's about much more. We're going to talk about your "why" and get down to what motivates you. We'll learn the specifics of what distracts you, and build habits of choosing well. Then I'll give you some tools to use. Beyond the tools, we are going to develop rhythms and realistic systems to help you stay on this path towards savoring life, living intentionally, and making room for what matters most to you.

My hope is that you will find your personalized way to a simpler and more fulfilling life. I'm not much into one size fits all, so I encourage you to take the pieces of what I offer that fit you and use them your way.

Putting someone else's idea of time management on top of your personality and lifestyle might feel like trying to fit into your old wedding dress or your dad's loafers. Even the best of things aren't meant for everyone in every season. That's why we are going to work on tailoring the reclaiming of your time to meet your needs and preferences.

You will walk away from this book with a greater self-awareness, some real motivation based on your own personal life purpose, and a set of tools to choose from to live out your priorities.

To help you remember what stands out to you as you read, I have provided a page at the end of each chapter for you to answer a few questions and jot down your thoughts while they are still fresh.

Often within a month of reading a book we forget the gist of what we gleaned. I'm hoping you can leave yourself a breadcrumb trail to return to so you can put what you learn here into action.

Three Ways to Approach The Book

I know you are busy. Because of that I want to give you three options as to how to get the most out of *Slow Down, Mama!*

1. Read the whole book. I'd love for you to read every living word I've written here. You will find tools and encouragement throughout. If that fits you, carry on. With 31 short chapters, you can read one in five minutes a day and finish the entire book in a month!

2. Sometimes it helps to go through a book with a group. If you want, gather friends or women from your church to support one another as you read. You can find group study guides and other free resources at: https://pattyhscott.com/slowdownmama/

3. Are you a skimmer? I've got you covered. In chapters three through six you will be able to identify the roots of what's keeping you busy. After each root cause I share the recommended chapters in the book you can skip forward to read. You can always come back to read more later.

However you approach the book, my prayer is that you will find inspiration and tools to live more intentionally while making room for what matters most.

TABLE OF CONTENTS

TABLE OF CONTENTS

"Beware the barrenness of a busy life."
~ Socrates

Chapter One

Running on Empty

I wore busy like a badge of honor. Up until about ten years ago, my overpacked schedule and lopsided priorities seemed normal. I didn't think it could be any other way. I believed the "good life" would come through my accomplishments, amazing organizational skills, and the "yes" answers I gave to any and every request.

An unacknowledged lie drove me to pursue something I already possessed, but didn't know was mine – my own value. Like a woman bounding down a street lined with potholes, I raced past empty places within me, hoping to outrun inadequacy, loneliness, and fear.

I held myself to unbelievable standards. Getting it right was my way of keeping my private inner pain at bay. My perfectionistic performance brought accolades I craved. Outside approval shored up my shaky sense of self-worth.

I see all this clearly now, from my rear-view mirror. At the time, however, I didn't stop to feel or evaluate how I was living. I merely kept running on empty. The people most precious to me often got the dregs of what I had left to give. Things were unmanageable, but that only meant I needed to try harder, do better, and plan more effectively.

The Busyness of Motherhood

I went from being an overwhelmed graduate student with a full-time job, to living the hectic lifestyle of an entrepreneurial mom with an infant and a foster child. My newborn son's round-the-clock needs consumed me. I felt like I was constantly either nursing him or changing his diapers, always hoping to somehow squeeze in a much-needed shower.

Meanwhile, our foster daughter had demanding emotional needs and a visitation schedule with her biological parents to maintain. My sporadic spiritual nourishment during this season mostly came from the occasional verse I managed to grasp as I cruised through the kitchen to read from the Bible I kept propped open on the cookbook stand.

The early years of motherhood pull a new mom in numerous directions. My overdeveloped sense of responsibility made me believe I could take on fostering, leading church events, and managing my part time job while maintaining a calm center.

The First Brake Pedal

When my oldest son was only two years old, a group of women decided they wanted to do a summer Bible Study together and invited me to co-lead them. They chose the study we would pursue together. To my astonishment, I found myself preparing lessons centered around "Beating Busyness"[1].

This short, eight-session study came power-packed with wisdom. For a girl who barely ever said no, the irony of leading this particular subject was not lost on me. Dutifully, I determined to engage with the material for the sake of the women in this group. God has His ways of leading us to our most needed lessons, even if He has to arrange for us to teach the very thing we need to learn.

One of the most poignant and lasting takeaways for me from this study was the chapter called "Why Am I So Busy?" I'll tell you right now, this was a question I actually had never really paused to entertain.

The term FOMO (Fear of Missing Out) hadn't been popularized yet, so many of us do-gooders and yes-girls simply went on burning ourselves out without ever asking ourselves why we were so busy or what we could do to make things different.

That study cracked through my veneer. God set my feet on the path of moving me from crazy-busy to a life lived with intention. Along the way He met me in those hollow places to bring healing as only He can.

Not Alone

As I grew towards sanity and wholeness, I started becoming aware of a trend in conversations between moms. The topic naturally drifted to a common feeling of overwhelm. It seems most of us assumed this simply came with the territory.

In fact, just this week a woman asked me what book I was writing. I told her about *Slow Down,*

Mama! She said, "Who has time to slow down?" We both laughed. So many of us long to simplify our lives, yet feel trapped in our whirlwind of commitments and activities.

I think there are two types of busyness. On one hand we can be occupied with all the right things – full, yet content and sane. On the other hand, we can be overly busy. In this overwhelming busyness, we take on more than we ought. We also stay involved and say yes for all the wrong reasons. In the coming chapters we're going to examine six of the biggest root causes of busyness.

My hope is you and I will to continue to choose lives full of purpose while minimizing the frenzied life that comes from overfilling.

Coming Unglued

The study we went through that summer asked hard questions. As we continued to look at various roots of our busyness, I squirmed with internal discomfort. It's one thing to intellectually know you are busy. It's entirely another to open the curtain to reveal what's really driving the heart behind all the frenetic activity.

Many years later, while I was writing this book, I gave a rough copy of the first three chapters to another published writer I respect. What you hold in your hands today has multiple revisions due to the interaction I had with her. As she read through, she asked me what it felt like to live the overly busy lifestyle I used to live. I shared my heart.

Tears came as I remembered the pain of living so wrung out and constantly depleted. I finally responded, "I wanted all this. I wanted everything I have gained by slowing down. I wanted to know I was worth loving for myself; that I mattered."

She sat back and smiled like a surgeon seeing the patient successfully come out from under anesthesia. Our conversation brought me right back to those days. The raw feelings flooded me all these years later. I needed the reminder of how it felt to live on hyper-overdrive. That day amplified my passion for the message of *Slow Down, Mama*.

Why You Are Here

You may not be in up to your neck, running yourself ragged while forgetting important events and commitments. Perhaps you aren't missing the people and moments you most want to savor. Maybe you are just a little overextended or you feel the need to slow down to make more of your life. Much of what I am writing will apply to you even if you don't suffer from the extremes of overextending yourself as I did.

I share my experience here to let you know I understand. I comprehend what life feels like when we are hopelessly busy. I have been taken from that place to an entirely new way of living. We don't have to settle for the hamster wheel.

Before we look at the roots of our busyness, we need to spark our hearts and ignite our "why." When you know the reason you want to slow down, you will be motivated to do what it takes to get there. Let's start by talking about what matters most.

Make This Chapter Mine:

After reading Chapter One, what stands out that I want to remember?

Do I relate to any of the experiences Patty shared?

Are there changes I already feel inspired or motivated to make?

What support do I need to make or maintain these changes?

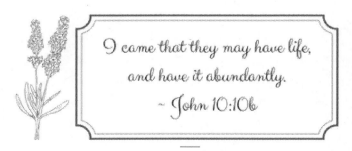

I came that they may have life, and have it abundantly.

~ John 10:10b

"If you should happen to catch a glimpse
of what really matters in life, regard it with care."
~ Rachel Macy Stafford

Chapter Two

What Matters Most

When our first-born, Jordan, was three months old and our foster daughter had just come to live with us, we moved to a new town. We contracted to build our house from scratch, which meant we laid the backyard grass, installed sprinklers, and planted a few sticks that would someday grow to be trees.

Our friends relocated to the same city because of a job change. They were house-hunting, so we offered for them to stay with us until they found a home of their own.

In due time our friends moved into their own home. The previous owners had left a big wooden playset. Our friends offered it to us if we wanted it. We hauled it into our yard and put it up in the far corner.

The Playset

Over the years, my sons have worn that playset out. They pretended to be pirates in the top deck, learned to make their way all the way across the rings, wove their own hammocks out of string, and spent hours mastering the trapeze.

One thing they both loved was engaging in a silly ritual with their dad when he arrived home from work or came out of the house. My husband would act like he was nonchalantly walking by the swing set. As my son swung forward, tapping my husband on the shoulder or chest, my husband would go reeling backwards as though he had been laid out, making all sorts of faces as he pretended to fall.

The boys and he never tired of this mayhem. I often relished these moments, watching from the kitchen window as I washed dishes, or as I sat reading a book on our back porch.

Time for a Change

Recently, our youngest son started taking tumbling classes. He does cartwheels in the living room, round-offs in the back yard, and eagerly awaits opportunities to go to the neighbor's for a chance to flip on their trampoline.

One week he mentioned, "I want a trampoline of our own." My husband and sons were all in on this idea. It was obvious where the trampoline would have to go – the back corner of the yard where the playset has lived for over sixteen years. An integral piece of my boys' childhood would have to come down, and with it an era in our family would come to a close.

The following Saturday my husband came through the house with his tools and headed out to dismantle the playset. Before he started demolition, I cajoled my youngest son into swinging one last time. I snapped pictures of him play kicking his dad while my husband staggered back in exaggerated defeat.

I retreated to the house and remained busy the rest of the day. I couldn't bear to watch the end of this childhood tradition. So much more felt torn down. Had I spent enough time pushing the boys on that swing? Had I made as many picnic lunches as I could have for them to eat up on the top deck? Had I spent enough time pausing to watch when they called out, "Mom, look!"? Had I savored their childhood well enough?

The Treasure

Though I have been at this business of intentional living for years, something about that playset coming down brought everything into a laser focus. We will never get a rewind button on the precious moments in each given day. The people we cherish most are here with us. One day they grow up, and even though we remain connected, we never recapture the past.

The time to invest in them is now. The day to eat up the goodness of our relationship is today. I don't want to expend my life accomplishing more tasks. I want to invest my time in the people and purposes that matter most. I know you do too.

If my swing set story leaves you feeling a pang of regret, I want you to hear me. Taking the valuable moments you have left in life and wasting them on more remorse would be a tragedy. My message isn't about what we have missed. I want us to stop here, open our eyes, and realize the treasure we have left. Let's turn a corner in our lives and live with less regret from here forward.

Make This Chapter Mine:

After reading this chapter, what stands out that I want to remember?

Do I have a vision (or even an inkling) of why I want to live more intentionally?

Are there changes I already feel inspired or motivated to make?

What support do I need to make or maintain these changes?

Only let each person lead the life that the Lord has assigned to him, and to which God has called him.
~ 1 Corinthians 7:17

*"I wanted to figure out why I was so busy,
but I couldn't find the time to do it."*
— Todd Stocker

Chapter Three

Busy Doing All the Things

For years I told myself I had control. I claimed to choose to be busy. Thinking I could handle more than most people, I took on ministry, work, family, and friendship. I didn't want to waste my life. To me, busyness hallmarked a life of significance.

What I ended up with was a frazzled and aching heart and many unsatisfied relationships. The fallout of my busyness looked like a scene after a natural disaster. As I dug deeper, I discovered many reasons I kept saying yes when no would have been a healthier choice.

In this chapter and the next two we're going to look at a few of the main reasons we get caught in the snare of over-commitment. Then we will talk about how to change these habits of the heart. The first two root causes of busyness involve achievement and productivity.

Superwoman Syndrome

When I got my hair cut earlier this year, my youngest son exclaimed, "Mom, you look like Mrs. Incredible!" #Mom-win. As much as I admire Elastigirl, especially since all the stretch went out of this girl years ago, trying to be a superhero is a part of my past I hope I never revisit.

If you have Superwoman Syndrome your motto might be, "I've got this and I'll get yours too." You overestimate your capacity to take on projects, needs, and responsibilities. Underneath your cool exterior are beliefs like:

- This won't get done without me.

- I can manage; I don't need help.

- The quality will suffer if I'm not the one doing it.

While some people do have a greater capacity to manage stress or take on a longer to-do list, we all have God-given limitations on our time, talents, and treasure. We need to operate within those parameters, whatever they are.

When I was newly married, I would often make plans for the weekend. As I recounted my plans to my husband, he would patiently listen and then often comment something like, "Hun, I don't think we'll get all that done in one day," or "Driving from here to Pasadena takes an hour with good traffic. It doesn't seem like you factored the drive into your plan."

I would feel miffed and tell him not to worry, I had planned it all out. Thankfully, he's not one to gloat – at least not out loud. My Herculean plans regularly failed. I often ended up frustrated when we hadn't done it all.

If you suffer from Superwoman Syndrome, you are not alone. Our culture gives out kudos for doing too much. Even our Christian fellowship can give big pats on the back to the "godly woman" who wakes at 4:30am and gets to bed at midnight, keeps an immaculate home, volunteers in all the church events, and runs marathons for exercise.

She's the Proverbs 31 woman on steroids. While everyone else is rising up to call her blessed, she's passing out from exhaustion! Can I get an amen?

When I read Lysa TerKeurst's book, *The Best Yes*, I found so many practical tips to help me learn to choose well. She shares memorable examples from her own life as she teaches ways to know if a "yes" is best or a "no" is needed.

Whether you read her book or not, I suggest you take on the simple practice of noticing all the gate wide open yes answers you give in the coming week. Ask yourself why you said yes, and then look at what that yes cost you. Did you lose quiet time? Time with your family? Margin to breathe between activities? A bit of your inner calm?

As you start to examine your yes answers instead of simply allowing them to flow out freely, you will choose more carefully where your yes and no are given. This simple practice will bless you more than you know.

Hope exists for Superwoman. The solution will come in identifying your limitations – in time, talents, and treasures – and choosing to live within them. As we hone in on discovering our purpose, you will be able to discern more clearly what is yours and what belongs to others.

Learning your best yes answers and choosing to say no, or not now, to everything else will be the key to a more balanced and satisfying life for you.

As Jesus said, we need to let our yes be yes and our no be no.[1] How many of our yes answers should be no in order for us to be our very best and put our time and energy towards what matters most?

Get-er-Done Girl

Much like the Superwoman, Get-er-Done Girl is able to juggle more than most. You will read about people pleasing in the next chapter. If Superwoman and People Pleaser had a baby, it would be Get-er-Done Girl. This woman needs affirmation from others and obtains approval or applause through performance. If you fall into this category, you often stay busy with tasks that aren't even yours.

I grew up with a disproportionate level of responsibility. For years, I felt all jobs were mine to complete. Unfinished business tends to call my name. I've had to consciously step back and evaluate whether something truly depends on me. When a task isn't mine, I need to leave it undone.

If you are a Get-Er-Done Girl, your ability to do so much makes you the go-to person for the job. The glow of others' reviews and their perception of you as competent fills your tank. Get-Er-Done Girl's self-esteem is all wrapped up in accomplishment and achievement.

You might keep to-do lists (color coded, of course) and get a little rush from checking off the boxes. You're known for going the extra mile and giving every project your all.

Even in parenting, you strive. You aim to be the best mom with the best kids. Competition may or may not be with others. You usually compete with yourself, trying to do your personal best.

Being able to accomplish a lot is a blessing. If you relate to Get-Er-Done Girl, know that your contributions are valuable. I encourage you not to make your sense of worth contingent on your productivity.

As a doer, you can end up like Martha, Lazarus' sister. She was so busy with all the things. Mary sat and rested, listening to Jesus. Martha prided herself on accomplishment and resented those who didn't do their share. Yet, Jesus praised Mary for doing the "only needful thing," – connecting to Him. Make sure you pause from all you're doing to be still and connect with God in personal ways.

A great resource for overcoming your workaholic or go–go–go tendencies is the book *Sabbath Keeping* by Ruth Haley Barton. In the book, Ruth shares about her own busy life and how she learned to set time aside for rest and refreshment. You also may benefit from the ministry of Unhurried Living. Gem and Alan Fadling have devoted their lives to helping others learn to slow and make space for God. If you relate to Get–Er–Done Girl or Superwoman, you will especially benefit from the chapters on making room for rest (Chapters 16–19).

We Get–Er–Done girls need to share the load with others. We need to ask ourselves if a job is best done by us or left undone. Just because things will fall apart doesn't mean we are the one to hold them together. Only One sustains the universe. I'm not it. Neither are you.

As Lysa TerKeurst says, "God is a master at providing just the right thing in just the right timing".[2] It's okay to leave a blank for Him to fill – especially if He isn't calling you to be the one to fill it.

Make This Chapter Mine:

After reading this chapter, what stands out that I want to remember?

How have I surrendered to busyness as my normal state of life?

How do I relate to Superwoman Syndrome or Get-Er-Done Girl?

What solutions do I want to put in place to help change my habits?

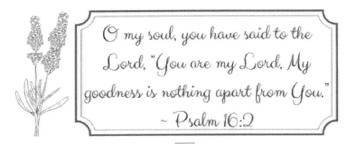

O my soul, you have said to the Lord, "You are my Lord. My goodness is nothing apart from You."
~ Psalm 16:2

"People-pleasers feel they must constantly be performing acts of service to others to gain acceptance. That requires a lot of work, effort, and energy."
— Eddie Capparucci

Chapter Four
Busy Making You Happy

Have you ever sworn something didn't bother you? I used to profess to my family that I could care less what others thought of me. Years of self-searching revealed my deep need for acceptance. I lived so much of my life unaware of how deeply I needed you to like me. I was driven to all sorts of madness in the name of approval seeking.

To this day, I can find myself inadvertently picturing someone when I'm choosing my outfit for the day, thinking something like, "What will they think of this shirt?" When I catch my thoughts, I replace them with, "What do I think of this?" Old habits die hard – and then resurrect and must be slain!

Let's look at three seemingly "other-centered" reasons why we stay busy and fail to slow down to a pace that gives us peace: people pleasing, avoiding loneliness, and a fear of missing out.

People Pleasing

Early in my work life I had a demanding job as a program director of a large center for people with disabilities. I worked for a woman who drew no distinction between personal life and time on the clock. She expected jobs to be done regardless of the unrealistic encroachment into our lives as employees. To fail her meant to face her disapproval and ultimately her wrath. More than one person had lost their job for being reasonable and refusing to go above and beyond for the workplace.

In my early 20s you probably could have looked up the term *people pleaser* and found my photo smack under the definition. I was the poster child for doing things to make you happy.

Let's unveil this ugly defect just a tad more. I wasn't really aiming to please you as much as I was protecting myself. Disappointing you unnerved me. I couldn't stand being disliked, or worse, rejected, so I would go to any lengths to keep you satisfied.

I was known to stay overnight at my boss' home working on projects until past midnight, waking the next morning to borrow clothes from her so I could go to work in something other than yesterday's outfit. Psycho, I know.

If you suffer from people pleasing, your approach to life could be summed up by the Burger King slogan, "Have it your way!" You also may relate to a few of these common thoughts of people pleasers:

- If I act nice, work hard, achieve, and get it right, I will be loved, belong, or be given a place of value.

- I'm afraid to say "no" or set limits.

- I often say "yes" when I don't want to.

- If I do something wrong, offend people, fail, slack off, or make a mistake, I will be rejected, excluded, or unloved

- I picture people's reactions when I consider my choices.

- If my choice will potentially make others unhappy, I change my course of action.

In the Beating Busyness study people pleasing is described this way:

> *We people pleasers can sniff out even the slightest hint of anger or disappointment, and this acute sense triggers a "yes" to fend it off.* [1]

Living to please others wears us out. What happens when two people you love have conflicting desires? You can't please both of them. You can end up constantly torn trying to be all things to all people. When someone says, "Jump!" and we ask, "How high?" we are out of touch with the true source of our own purpose.

God alone created us. We were created by Him, for Him. Let that sink in. If God has a purpose for you, and you spend your time pleasing people, you are at least partially missing out on the life He desires for you – the abundant life of freedom.

My friend Dawn was covering our Facebook Intentional Motherhood Community one week while I was taking a fast from social media. Dawn was gracious enough to post her thoughts the week she was substituting.

In her poignant message, Dawn spoke about over-commitment. Feeling her time would be open for the summer she said "yes" to a lot of opportunities. It wasn't long before she was feeling overwhelmed. She began praying, asking God what she needed to remove from her plate. The response she received surprised her.

God prompted Dawn to think about why she took on so much in the first place. She realized that volunteering gave her accolades. Face it, as moms, we aren't usually thanked for our time and sacrifice.

As Dawn shared on the live video, she said, "The word God brought to me was *enough*. What you do is *enough*. In fact, being a mom is an amazing privilege. It's the most important job you can have."

If you are prone to extend yourself beyond your limits because you receive kudos and affirmation, I get it. Dawn gets it. So many of us can relate. The world is set up for us to seek "likes" and "shares" as validation that our contribution was noticed and approved.

I love Dawn's heart. She's a treasure. This wisdom of asking herself why she was overcommitted followed by the beauty of realizing she didn't need to say "yes" to everyone to be valued is sheer gold. I hope it blesses you if you are prone to stay too busy because of approval seeking.

People pleasing doesn't have to be your lifestyle. It's going to take some courage to learn to give the difficult answer no, and to express your own thoughts as you choose what you think is best. To do this, you are going to have to become more attached to what God thinks of you and less dependent upon what people think of you.

My own growth in this area has taken years. Along the way I disappointed several friends. In a few cases, I had to deal with rejection. People who were used to me acquiescing to their way didn't always like me developing a spine.

As I processed the pain and licked my wounds for a bit, God showed me how deeply I had been entrenched in relying on outward opinion as a measure of my worth. Ultimately God used those circumstances to grow me into a person who lives less dependent upon what others think of me and more sure of my own mind.

While loving others and being a blessing are traits Jesus calls us to cultivate, we need to learn to discern between serving from a heart of love and pleasing from a heart of fear. If you are a people pleaser, you can grow. The book *Boundaries* by John Townsend and Henry Cloud has been invaluable to me in this process. I also recommend David Hawkins' book *When Pleasing Others is Hurting You.* You will also benefit from my chapter on setting boundaries, Chapter Fifteen.

Only the Lonely

I remember sitting with a group of leaders in women's ministry one year. We had set aside a day to prepare for the coming season of ministry in our church. The woman leading us taught about abiding. During her talk she shared her blissful experiences of solitude and silence.

At that point in my life, I had begun practicing times of solitude in a more formal way. I only partially related to her sharing. My experience when I sat still with no agenda felt more uncomfortable than divine. I sometimes experienced loneliness. At other times I felt distracted, idle, or bored.

Much like my experience of solitude, the practice of saying no can leave a vacuum of time. Avoiding loneliness can keep a girl's dance card full for all the wrong reasons. If you would rather be on the go, out with people, and full of things to do than be alone, you may find yourself avoiding slowing down by packing your life full of people and activities. The question is, do these events and relationships matter most to you?

If you avoid loneliness, you are not alone. (See what I did there?) When I polled people on Facebook as to why they stay busy and say yes when they feel like saying no, a good number of them mentioned connecting with people or avoiding being uncomfortable alone as part of the reason.

Introverts are not always exempt from this pitfall of busyness. If you find yourself filling your private time with meaningless activity, you may be avoiding loneliness or other uncomfortable emotions. How many hours of

Candy Crush Saga, binging on Netflix, or Instagram scrolling really help you unwind and be filled? Those activities aren't bad in moderation. When you find yourself returning to them for hours on end, it might be time to ask yourself what is driving you towards mind candy.

We all do some of this at least a little bit. Consider the popularity of social media. We can log on, participate in a conversation thread, or sit back and passively read through others' discussions. Most of the time we aren't building meaningful relationships while we engage online.

I know exceptions exist. Some very sweet connections with other writers and bloggers have come through years of supporting one another online. I'm very careful, though, to ensure online time does not trump my in-person friendships or family connections.

There's simply no way around loneliness, except to go through the discomfort of learning to enjoy solitude. Like any other emotion, when we avoid it by numbing out, it doesn't merely go away. Like an untreated wound, disowned emotions fester. We need to become courageous enough to feel. That involves refusing to fill in the blanks with busyness.

I will tell you one thing that has made me more willing to delve into solitude than any other factor in my life: being a mom. Remember when you wanted to be popular in high school? Well, now you are. Everyone wants a piece of you, Mama. Motherhood has made me crave some serious alone time like nobody's business!

If you find yourself resisting being alone, you can ease into solitude by practicing more life-giving activities in your private moments. Jesus often withdrew to quiet places alone to pray and be with the Father. You don't have to jump into this with both feet. You can make small movements to cultivate a habit of solitude.

You may want to take up a hobby when you are alone such as drawing, reading, or spending time in your garden. Be careful to make your pastime relaxing and open-ended so you don't create one more thing on a to-do list while trying to overcome what keeps you from living more intentionally.

A great book to help you as you walk through

recovering from avoiding loneliness is Lysa TerKeurst's *Uninvited: Living Loved When You Feel Less Than, Left Out and Lonely.* Chapters Twelve and Fourteen in this book will be very important for you if evading loneliness is at the root of your busyness.

FOMO (Fear of Missing Out)

A close cousin to avoiding loneliness is "FOMO" (Fear of Missing Out). The difference with FOMO is we usually feel insignificant and dread being overlooked. As a result, we don't want to miss anything for fear the world will go on without us. We hinge our value on being noticed and involved. Pulling back can mean loss of opportunity, enjoyment, or connection. Most of all, it can mean loss of significance.

When I was in graduate school, my husband and I were dating. One day he asked me to meet him on the beach in the town where we lived. He and some friends of ours were planning a game of volleyball on the sand. I had a huge part of my Masters' thesis to complete that day, but I just couldn't bear to miss this time with all my friends.

When I got to the beach, only my boyfriend and

another friend had arrived, so I walked to the edge of the water and stood looking out over the ocean. A massive weight pressed on my shoulders as I realized what I should be doing – finishing my paper!

It was in that moment it dawned on me. I had come to the beach because I couldn't stand missing out on any fun. I didn't want all my friends to play volleyball while I was stuck in my apartment writing. My awareness rolled over me in waves. I started seeing how much of my life was spent saying yes to so many things simply to ensure I was included.

That day was a turning point in my understanding. From then on, I said more no answers, even though it took me years to beat the busy patterns stemming from other roots in my heart.

So, Miss Fomo, let's face it. We won't do it all. We won't go all the places, have all the relationships, complete all the projects, or read all the books. Knowing this deeply helps us consider what we will do. Since we have to make a choice, let's get picky and choose well.

If you suffer from FOMO, a few key practices

and changes in perspective can help you. As we discuss slowing down and savoring, choose some of the methods to incorporate into your own life. One of the greatest habits I have engaged in to overcome FOMO has been an attitude of gratitude. If you learn to want what you have, you will, by default have what you want. Appreciating all that is good around you, in your life, and in your friendships, brings perspective.

A great book on cultivating gratitude is *One Thousand Gifts*, by Ann Voskamp. If you struggle with a fear of missing out, you may be encouraged by Chapter 14 where I talk about how to savor your relationships, and Chapter 19 where I share how to be content in our life as is.

God has told us in the familiar Psalm 23, "The Lord is my Shepherd, I shall not want." That phrase means, I don't lack what I need. God provides it for me. Like aimless sheep who don't know any better, we pine away for the allure of the grass just outside our fence. We are sure it is sweeter and better somehow. Learning to see through eyes of gratitude shifts us to living within our fence and ultimately brings us contentment.

Make This Chapter Mine:

After reading this chapter, what stands out that I want to remember?

How have I lived for the approval of others?

How have I stayed busy to avoid loneliness or other difficult emotions?

Have I allowed FOMO to keep me busy?

Am I now trying to win the approval of
human beings, or of God?
If I were still trying to please people,
I would not be a servant of Christ.
~ Galatians 1:10

*"One of the advantages of being disorganized
is that one is always having
surprising discoveries."*
~ A.A. Milne

Chapter Five

Busy with Loose Ends

We've talked so far about being busy carrying the weight of the world and about the kind of busyness that comes from our deep need for connection. The women who will relate to this chapter are more free-spirited. If you are easily distracted or you tend to be more low-key and kicked-back, this chapter is for you.

Just because you are chill and easygoing doesn't mean your life feels purposeful. Some of my most precious friends struggle with the kind of busy resulting from disorganization or a lack of focus. Though I'm more driven by nature, I can definitely put the *pro* in procrastination.

The Easy Way

I've had some women comment to me about

busyness, "I'm more of a relaxed type of person. I just do whatever is easiest." Since opposites attract, I'm surrounded by people who are very motivated by no-waves living. I think I gravitate to people who are more open-ended and easy going. Their willingness to do less and wait for outcomes has taught me much.

While my husband isn't a slacker at all, he invariably chooses the easier road. Sometimes this leads to us getting much needed rest. At other times, the easy road is filled with less satisfying or more unfocused activities.

Easy-road people tend to say yes to others because no seems like too much effort. Also, people who gravitate towards not making waves in life sometimes have a hard time discerning a clear vision as to what they want for themselves. Even if they do have that vision, the discipline of pursuing a dream can seem daunting.

If this is you, take heart. You were exactly the type of person I had in mind when I said I don't believe in a one size fits all time management approach. As you go through this book, I want to encourage you to be realistic.

The biggest tools you can incorporate into your

life are gaining support from people you trust and clarifying a really motivating "why." When you embrace your purpose, you will be willing to go after it – even in the slow and steady wins the race or scattered way that is your own.

Making the Harder Choice

Just this year, my sweet friend, Jessica, called me for some input. She needed to make a choice about how she was spending her time. Every May her church renews their ministry commitments. She was weighing out the option of continuing on in certain areas or letting go. As we talked, she discovered she was actually postponing a more difficult calling by staying engaged at church in this season.

Jessica and her husband became empty nesters only a few years ago. He really wants her time at home with him, yet sometimes when she has made that happen, he hasn't been available and Jessica has found herself asking why she set the time aside.

The immediate payoff of ministry outside the home had been involvement with girlfriends doing fun and rewarding activities. Leaving space open for her relationship with her husband and their joint ministry from home would take more work, faith, and patience to cultivate. It was the harder choice.

When Jessica realized her underlying motivation, she let go of her commitment to her church for this season and decided to be present for her husband and the outreach they could develop together.

One of the best things you can do as an "Easy Way" person is to surround yourself with gentle, encouraging friends who will ask you about your deepest goals and nudge you forward where you might naturally stall out.

You may benefit from the book *To Be Told: Know Your Story, Shape Your Future* by Dan Allender. In Chapters Seven and Eight I will guide you through defining your purpose. The processes in these two chapters will be important for you. You will also be especially blessed by Chapter Twenty-Four where I go into detail about productive decision making.

Details Schmeetails

Oh, my friend. I already love you. If you fall into the delightfully present personality who lives without much concern for details, the upside of who you are blesses so many.

My youngest son belongs to this tribe of people. He's the type who, when I say, "Did you clean your room?" will exuberantly respond, "Yes!" while missing entire piles of Legos and dirty clothes. He doesn't mean to leave his shoes at his friends' or to misplace his script for the play. He simply goes through life completely immersed in the moment and people around him.

I have learned a great deal from my sensitive, thoughtful, all-in boy. I've also witnessed the way this personality can become overwhelmed when it comes to meeting a deadline or staying organized. One of my friends who falls in this category jokes that she could hide her own Easter eggs. While that makes us all laugh, the downside to this free-spirited way of living is often the constant sense of disorganization and a feeling you can't catch up with all you need to accomplish.

I remember helping one friend organize her office. She asked me because she knew I would be a safe person. I'm here to help, not judge. Opening one drawer I found a stack of random envelopes. The majority of these were applications for Visa and Master Cards. "Are you applying for some credit?" I asked. She wasn't. The habit of stashing papers in case they were needed later meant filling drawers with piles of mystery mail.

The image of that drawer may not seem daunting. Factor in the difficulty she faced when she tried to find any significant document, a bill to be paid, or the phone number she had written on a post-it note. You get the picture. So much time in the life of a free-spirit isn't truly freed up.

When I asked my friend how her life felt, she confessed she often felt "less than" because she couldn't find things when she wanted. She teared up as she shared her heart. In this world where we measure worth by the way we organize our homes, my friend felt she had lost the race before she even entered. Her entire self-esteem took a hit because she struggled with external order.

This got my attention. My friend makes people laugh. She has a compassionate nature and opens her home to people readily. To hear her say she felt inferior because she couldn't organize a bunch of unwelcomed junk mail broke my heart.

Organization Just for You

While you may not need as many of the words I share in this book about finding passion and purpose, if you are disorganized by nature and tend to be an in-the-moment personality, you may benefit from the book *Organizing for the Creative Person: Right-Brain Styles for Conquering Clutter, Mastering Time, and Reaching Your Goals* by Dorothy Lehmkuhl. She presents an outside the box approach to organization for people who aren't served by traditional approaches. You will find more help in Chapter Twenty of this book where I discuss how to be intentional and carefree.

While I hope to give you some tools to try on to help you get a grip on your outer world, more than anything I hope you grasp this: You are like a breath of fresh air to all us driven personalities. We need you. You remind the rest of us how to savor life for all its goodness. Don't stop being the you God made you to be.

Make This Chapter Mine:

After reading this chapter, what stands out that I want to remember?

Have I pursued the easy way and let deeper desires go unnoticed?

Does my disorganization make me feel inferior to others?

What realistic solutions can help me accept the way I am designed while living with purpose?

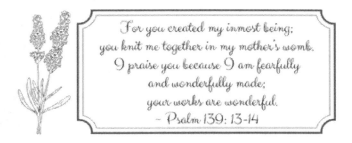

For you created my inmost being;
you knit me together in my mother's womb.
I praise you because I am fearfully
and wonderfully made;
your works are wonderful.
~ Psalm 139: 13-14

*"Perfectionism is the voice of the oppressor,
the enemy of the people. It will keep you cramped
and insane your whole life."*
~ Anne Lamott

Chapter Six
Nobody's Perfect

You may wonder what high standards have to do with too many yes answers and our inability to slow down. Let me share the story of our oldest son's "Surfer Birthday Party."

When Jordan turned three, we decided to host a party with 40 of our closest friends. Now, brides take a year to plan their weddings on average. I "only" spent four months preparing this epic celebration. From the homemade cabana (equipped with two hired teens to serve lunches) to the hand-painted standee with three cut out holes for photo ops, to the sand I got from a local rock and gravel supply place, this party was beyond over the top.

My mom flew in from Montana for the

momentous occasion. We spent the majority of her week with us prior to the party driving from store to store getting trimmings, ordering the cake and arranging for the rentals – for my three year old. You can insert your own eye roll here, or just borrow mine.

The night before the wedding, er, birthday bash, I was up until midnight because the royal frosting for the flip–flop cookies I was making as parting gifts wouldn't set the first time. I had to toss that batch and make a replacement, ice the cookies, and put them on themed plates with handmade "Life's a Beach" cards to thank each person for coming. Life for the perfectionist rarely resembles a beach.

Before you go all Rambo on me for putting down big birthday bashes, I'm not taking a stand against parties. I love a celebration. I totally enjoy putting on fantastic events. The thing was, my perfectionism drove me to single-handedly turn a three-year-old's party into a full-blown Hollywood production. Every detail had to be just right. This may have been fine had I no life. I do, however have a part-time job, ministry, motherhood, a home to maintain, a marriage (yes, he's still with me after all this), and numerous other things on my plate.

Executing a party of this magnitude wore me out. Although I loved all the creativity that went into it, in the end, I needed a beach vacation to get over the surfer birthday party!

Perfectionism doesn't know how to say "good enough." That party would have been just as lovely without homemade cookies to give away and hand-made invites and all the other over-the-top elements I put together. Perfectionism caused me to go further than necessary.

We're going to learn to let go of perfect. In exchange, you will find yourself in good company with the rest of humanity in the beautifully messy, incomplete parts of life.

Shedding the Straightjacket

Brene Brown, the famous social scientist and researcher, calls perfectionism a straightjacket.[1] When I heard that, I almost cried. Having suffered under the oppression of perfectionism for over half my life, I felt simultaneously understood and called out when I heard Brene's words. We can unbuckle the straightjacket and learn to live with so much less restraint.

If you are like me, the prospect of overcoming perfectionism scares the bejeepers right out of you. Is there a rule book to follow so we don't mess this up? Sorry, no. This process will rail against your inner need for order and predictability. I wouldn't go here if I hadn't been so very blessed by the risks I have taken to release the burden of rigorous perfectionism.

The Roots of Perfectionism

In her book *Hands Free Life*, Rachel Macy Stafford talks about "no pressure living" as compared to "self-induced pressures."[2] As I read her book, I asked myself what made me take on so many high-standards and push myself to always get things just so? We perfectionists need to take a step back and evaluate our measuring stick when it comes to defining success.

My need to get things just right stemmed from a painful place in my past. In my childhood several experiences shaped me. My parents thought the world of me. Somehow the message I received from them felt like I couldn't be lovable if I weren't perfect. In elementary school I skipped ahead a grade. My teachers loved me.

The other children saw me as an anomaly. I experienced heart-crushing teasing and bullying.

In my mind, if I could just be different than I was and get things right, I would avoid the pain of rejection. Poisonous seeds settled in the tender soil of my heart. From those seeds grew vines, choking out the freedom of self-expression. Instead of being quirky, not-so-perfect me, I began getting it right to fit in. Perfect was my protection. No wonder I fought hard to keep perfectionism going long after it served its purpose in my life.

In order to overcome perfectionism, I had to risk being "good enough." Sometimes our B minus effort is absolutely better than fine. I learned I could bring store-bought cookies to the bake sale. (They are baked, aren't they?) I started saying things like, "Sorry, I can't make it this time." I offered to do half a job and leave the rest to someone else. Learning to do less than 100% freed me up.

Getting comfortable with mess, delay, and loss of control may send us to therapy. That is quite alright. When I count my blessings today, my therapist often lands on the top-ten list, right alongside my spiritual director and some sweet mentoring friendships. I didn't grow in a straight line either. That's what imperfection looks like – wobbly, unpredictable, open-handed.

Reclining onto God

As I grew in trusting God, my deepening reliance spurred me to release more control. My perfectionism was fueled by the lie that I could manage life and outcomes. I feared letting go.

God seemed as demanding as everyone else I had known. I wanted to get it right for Him. Working with my mentor to unearth and heal my distorted views of God helped me bridge my doubt to develop what Charles H. Spurgeon calls a "recumbent relationship" with God.[3]

Isn't that beautiful? I picture leaning back on God with such confidence and rest that it feels like a chaise lounge. This shift didn't come overnight. It took years of testing God's reliability and allowing myself to be less-than-perfect to become comfortable in my own skin.

I still occasionally sink into perfectionism. When

I do, a red flag of warning goes up. When fear has gripped my heart again, I remind myself God is my Good Shepherd. He loves me as is. As I abide in the truth of His love and the grace of His presence, I allow the urge to "do perfect" to melt away.

Some Hope for Perfectionists

If you are a perfectionist, I wholeheartedly encourage you to read the book *Present Over Perfect: Leaving Behind Frantic for a Simpler, More Soulful Way of Living* by Shawna Niequist. The title says it all. Another great book is *The Control Freak: Coping with Those Around You, Taming the One Within* by Les Parrott. Not saying you are controlling of others ... just in case you know someone who is. I discuss perfectionism as it relates to our distractions, planning well, and habit formation in Chapters Twelve, Twenty, and Twenty-Seven.

I hesitate to suggest anything practical to a perfectionist. Knowing how we operate, we'll get busy healing and make our growth into a project, expecting ourselves to grow faster and more completely than anyone in the history of overcoming perfectionism.

That said, if you can do this with grace, I suggest you consider picking one area where you have expected too much from yourself. Think about ways you can reschedule, do less, cancel, split responsibility, delegate or otherwise change this obligation so it no longer feels like a burden. Lower your standard and give yourself a breather.

Most of all, abide in God's love. The more you know in the depths of your heart how treasured you are, the less you will feel the need to perform to unreasonable standards in order to gain worth. As Emily P. Freeman says in her book *A Million Little Ways*, "You are a gift worth offering."[4]

When our children bring us a gift they made from their own hands, it often begs the unspoken question, "Um, what is this?" The stapled and taped scraps of paper with scribbles come straight from their heart. Messy and uneven, their gift expresses all they are. Let's be like these children – bringing all the ragged edges and imbalanced realities of who we are as a part of the gift we fearlessly and openly give both God and the world.

Make This Chapter Mine:

After reading this chapter, what stands out that I want to remember?

How have I set unrealistic standards on myself?

What do I want to remember about perfectionism?

What solutions can I embrace to help myself let go of perfect? What support do I need?

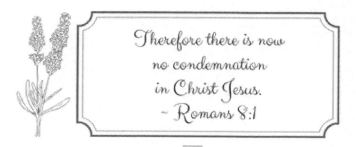

Therefore there is now
no condemnation
in Christ Jesus.
~ Romans 8:1

"Sow an act, and you reap a habit. Sow a habit and you reap a character. Sow a character and you reap a destiny."
— James Allen

Chapter Seven

What Do You Want to Be?

Have you ever read a time management or organization book that jumped right in assuming you were motivated to live with alphabetized cubbies and labeled canisters throughout your home? Those books are wonderful for people who already know why they want to systematize and streamline life. They also work well for people who compulsively clean and organize to avoid feeling out of control.

Often when I have read yet another book on organizing or time management is that I get gung-ho and put all the steps in place. Later I drop one habit or another. Within a month I'm back to my old ways. The good ideas don't always stick. You too?

Why does this happen? There are several reasons. Most of all, time management for its own sake isn't going to work. Like any habit change, we need to identify a motivating purpose that grips our heart and wake us up in the morning excited to move forward with intentional living.

Without roots in purpose, our burgeoning habits will end up in the overpopulated graveyard alongside so many unfulfilled New Year's Resolutions and failed Monday diet attempts.

Say Goodbye to the Past

When I was between four and five years old, I approached my mom in the kitchen to announce my goals for what I would be when I grew up. In all my boldness, I told her I was going to write books, speak to groups, and help people who were hurting. Amazingly, my life path (though it has veered and careened at times) ended up with me doing exactly those three things.

Most people are not as precocious about life mission. Even with that clarity, I wavered at times. Minutia distracted my focus causing me to miss out on priceless opportunities. I've lost myself in activity and passed up deeper

connections with people. That's my history –
both the lucid nature of my goals and the ease
with which I have drifted.

You have a history too. Let's just put a pin in
that – sort of like the "You Are Here" point on a
map. So, you've ambled along with less
intention and purpose than you might have
liked. You've taken on responsibilities that
weren't yours. You allowed your "yes" to come
rolling out when it should have been a "no." Let
your bygones be bygones. Wipe the slate clean
today and go about the business of looking
forward to the intentional life you crave and
were made to live.

Determining Direction

In order to live with purpose, you are going to
have to ask yourself some basic questions about
what moves you and brings meaning to your
life. For fun, I asked the three men in my life
this question: "What is most important in life?"

My husband and older son were busy repairing
bike tires on the driveway while my youngest
son wheeled around the street in front of our
home on his newly repaired bicycle. He shouted
his answer while raising both hands off the

handlebars: "Friends and God!" to which my oldest added, "My Family." My husband looked me in the eyes and said, "God and Family."

Well now. Be still my heart. They are my why. Those three guys and my God make my heart skip beats and give me deep purpose. The question remains, "Do I live like that is true?"

One of the best tools I've ever found for this process of determining purpose came from Tsh Oxenrider's book *Organized Simplicity*. She suggests writing a purpose statement.[1]

You may be thinking I'm going all type-A on you here, but bear with me. Without being too cliché, can I remind you that you buy a ticket when you go on a trip? You don't log onto Orbitz or CheapFlights and say, "Give me a Ticket." You need to have a destination in mind. Beyond that you usually book a hotel and plan at least some sort of loose agenda.

If you do that for a week's getaway, how much more valuable will it be for you to develop an itinerary and desired destination for your life? Just like any trip, unforeseen adventures and changes in plan should be expected. Still, we need to start with some idea of where we are headed and what we'll do when we get there.

I want to help you along in this process. I'm not going to use Tsh's list. I have my own. I do encourage you to purchase her book or borrow it from the library. It's one of those I go back to regularly for a tune up.

On a slight side note, I have a hint for those of you whose husbands aren't super into goal setting. My husband is a captive audience on our summer trips out to the coast. While he drives the two hours, I can ask him questions like those on Tsh's list or the one I am giving you here. My husband and I have crafted and refined our family purpose statement several times in the past fifteen years.

Before we look at external goals such as where we want to invest our time and what kinds of activities we want to pursue, I want to ask you to think about something more foundational. A few years ago on my birthday, I decided I wanted my "to be" list to exceed my "to do" list, and my "to love" list to surpass them both. We'll get to your "to love" list in Chapter Fourteen, but for now, let's tackle your goals in the other two areas.

Your To-Be List

Back in the 1700s, Benjamin Frank[...]
now-famous list of character quali[...]
wanted to grow towards. At the young age of
20, he wrote out 13 traits of moral excellence
and defined each with a little blurb.[2] He then
devised a plan to work on each virtue for a
focused week, for thirteen weeks straight, and
then repeated the process routinely – one trait
per week. While you may not want such a
systematic approach, I want you to consider the
idea of concentrating on character development
within your life purpose.

So, let's answer some questions:

- What are some of your greatest strengths
  and talents? (Ask friends for input if you
  can't pin these down on your own).
- What are some character traits you admire in
  others?
- If you could change one habit you now have,
  what would it be?
- If you could be remembered for a
  specific way you interacted with others,
  what would that be?

Which virtues do you admire or want to cultivate most?

Don't succumb to the temptation to breeze by these questions. Take a minute to jot something down in your notebook or on your phone about this. If you go to the website provided at the end of the book, I have free handouts to help you devote more thought to questions about your character.

As you look at these questions, words like "gentleness, courage, integrity, compassion, vision, self-sacrifice, honor, patience, self-control, leadership, devotion, or initiative" may have come to mind. Take a moment to write some of your key words down and make your own definitions of what they mean to you personally. If an image comes to mind as to what that trait would look like as you live it out, note that as well. Are you starting to get a feel for your "to be" list?

Let's talk about how this plays into your daily life. One of my goals is to become increasingly gentle. I have a personal reason for that being a priority in my life. My parents both lacked self-control when they were angry. Their inability to contain their frustration and remain gentle caused me a great deal of pain as a child.

Coming into adulthood, I found myself easily irritated and edgy. This wasn't a natural part of how I was as a child, but I learned patterns in my home until they became a part of how I reacted to stress or loss of control.

One day my son came home from preschool with a hand painted shell. Inside the shell were the words, "Let your gentleness be evident to all. The Lord is near."[2] I felt like this was a personal invitation for me to grow into something that was lacking in my life and heart.

I made that portion of scripture a life verse and purposed to become what it conveyed. As a result, I set aside time to spend with my mentor digging up painful memories, processing them, and moving forward. I practiced new habits whenever I found myself feeling on edge. While I'm nowhere near "graduation" in this growth process,

I've come miles from where I started. Slowing down has been key in my movement towards gentleness. The more time I have with margin around the edges, the less frantic I feel. I am able to complete the list of tasks I give myself and the commitments I make to others because I know my limitations and live within them. Since I'm not spread too thin trying to be all things to all people, I have a buffer to my anger and frustration. I am able to be increasingly gentle because my fuse isn't right at the nub.

I also have focused on the second half of that verse. The more I have practiced awareness of the reality of God's presence, the less anxious and agitated I am. Because I know I am being guarded and guided, I don't feel like I have to run the show. All of this contributes to greater gentleness on my part. I'm sure you can see how this will also work with your "to be" list. Once we set our sights on a virtue, we can arrange our lives to facilitate our growth towards it.

I hope you put some time into thinking through your "to be" list and asking yourself what needs to shift in order for you to move towards cultivating the character traits you most want to develop in yourself.

<u>*Make This Chapter Mine:*</u>

After reading this chapter, what stands out that I want to remember?

Do I have a sense of what I would like to become – character traits I want to cultivate?

If I had to pick one trait to hone in on first, which would it be?

As I consider this trait, what do I need to change to help myself grow towards it?

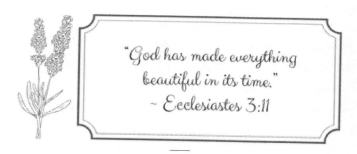

"God has made everything beautiful in its time."
~ Ecclesiastes 3:11

"Live your everyday extraordinary!"
~ Charles F. Glassman

Chapter Eight

Living on Purpose

We all have areas of life that bring us great joy. Sometimes we are drawn to certain types of activities or needs we see in the world. Examining these can help us clarify our purpose.

I have a friend who has an unusual commitment and care for elderly people. She takes her children to nursing homes weekly and visits with people who have no other companions. If you see her at church, she's almost always sitting with one of the senior members. It's just her thing.

Now, much like you, she doesn't just have one thing. She also loves gardening and cooking and art. Finding your life's purpose usually won't feel exclusive. You can have passions for a number of things. In fact, you probably do.

I have found that most of us have a deep purpose, whether we are in touch with it or not. Our life mission comes out in a thousand little ways – like light reflecting off a diamond in facets. When we determine our deeper "why," we find our inner motivation flowing into and permeating all the "what" of our life. The clearer I have become about what makes my heart beat – what I was made to be and how I uniquely reflect God into the world – the more each thing I do becomes infused with meaning.

Showing Off

Your life isn't a string of random unrelated events. Your life is a contiguous story. Dan Allender says, "In our story God shows us what He's up to and what He wants us to be about."[1] If you take time to look back over your life, you will start to see themes and patterns. You can see what makes you unique.

The first question of the Westminster Catechism asks, "What is the chief end of man?" to which the memorized response is, "Man's chief end is to glorify God, and to enjoy him forever."[2] To glorify God means to show Him off and give Him honor. The bottom line for each of us it to use our lives to point to the goodness of God. We each reflect God uniquely. Your life reveals Him, and you do that in a way no one else can.

When you look back over your history, you see tragedy and triumph, specific gifting, and one-of-a-kind experiences. Your purpose is revealed as you look back over the landscape of your life and see yourself in the story God and you have written so far.

A High Calling

I am the only mom and wife in our home. No one can fill my shoes. If I abandon my responsibility to pursue other callings, I would leave the helm without a skipper. The doesn't mean I can't have other interests and ministries in addition to being a mom. I believe I can, and most of us should.

As moms, we always need to hold in our minds the deep purpose and mission of motherhood so we don't allow other activities and passions to divert us in ways that harm our ability to be present and involved as a mom and wife.

God knows the dilemma this seems to cause.

Believe me, there are ways to c
purpose while pouring yourse
motherhood. Let's just be sur
priority of investing in our far
belongs by remembering our
lives of those precious to us.

What's the Purpose?

As we think about life purpose, I want you to
consider some key questions. Try to set aside
thoughts of what limits you for now.

Take time to really explore freely:
- Who are you living for?
- What makes your heart beat?
- What do you want to be remembered for?
- What will you hope to look back on?
- What do you dream you'll do?
- What makes up your bucket list?
- What did you love to do as a child?
- If you had an afternoon free, what would you do? A week? A month?
- What do you not want to miss in life?

Greg McKeown, author of *Essentialism*, suggests
we ask ourselves three "advanced search
questions" to clarify direction and purpose:
- What am I deeply passionate about?

...taps my talent? ...d what meets a significant need in the world? [3]

Ask a Friend

Another great tool as you hone in on your life purpose is to ask people who know you well some key questions. As I was refining the focus of my blog a few years ago, I sent out a question to ten close friends. I got the idea from Jeff Goins of Tribe Writers.

I asked these people what talent or knowledge I have that seems amazing to others, but is natural or easy to me. What came back, my reflection in the eyes of those who know me best, was enlightening. Their answers helped guide me onto the path that led to writing the book you are holding now.

Can you think of five or ten people who know you well? Take a minute to send off an email asking them what they see as your skills and areas of expertise. You may even ask, "If you had to define something you think I was born to do, what would it be?" When they answer, take note of what they see in you. How do their answers resonate with what you already know about yourself? How can you work their input into your life purpose?

One little note I need to add here. Please don't make this task into some sort of burden that keeps you up at night. If you are drawing blanks, it might be you are putting too much pressure on yourself. If you are a perfectionist, let's aim for 75% of this goal rather than 100%.

How about breaking this process down a tad and making a purpose statement for the rest of this year, or in a specific area of your life such as your marriage or parenting. Don't make determining purpose so daunting that you can't surmount it. This process is meant to be a tool to free you up, not shackles to keep you unable to move forward. Capiche?

Purpose as a Filter

I've come to see our purpose in life as a sort of filter. Once we determine what matters most to us – what we want to spend our precious days, hours, and minutes doing – we can sift our choices through our priorities. Life becomes far more slow and simple when we are able to distinguish what matters and align the way we spend our time with those very significant relationships and pursuits.

Let me give you an example. In this season I am focusing on a few choice friendships, my mastermind group, my marriage, and my children (not in that order). My primary task is to get this book written well and to create courses and coaching opportunities to accompany the book.

As I go through my weeks, people invite me to participate in activities. I have been requested to speak or serve in various capacities. Even writing opportunities have come my way. Because I have clarified my purpose for this season, I am able to sort through choices relatively easily by asking myself if they line up with the purpose and people I have prayerfully prioritized for this stretch of time.

I'll go into this more thoroughly in Chapter Twenty-One when I talk about 90-day planning. For now, I only want to give you an idea of how useful knowing your purpose can be. If I'm going to Texas (one of my favorite places to visit), I'm not looking into tours through the Eiffel Tower, Statue of Liberty, or Rock-and-Roll Hall of Fame. Instead, I check how far it is to drive to a quaint town in the Hill Country from Houston. Why? My focus has been defined by my planned destination. Purpose helps refine my choices so I don't end up overwhelmed by irrelevant options.

Going Through the Back Door

Sometimes we can figure out what we want by asking ourselves pointed questions. When these direct approaches don't work, it can be helpful to go at things backwards. The next list of questions (the last list in this chapter) are meant to help you weed out what your purpose is not. When you eliminate what is "not for me" or what is "getting in the way of what matters most," you will be able to have a much clearer view of what's left (aka your true purpose).

- What things am I doing to live up to an image or the expectations of others?
- What do I dread doing?
- When I look at my habits and schedule and draw a trajectory out from each one, do I like where I am headed? In other words, if I change nothing, will I end up where I want or hope to go and where God is calling me?

81

- What in my current lifestyle makes me most stressed and brings out the worst in me?
- What consumes my time that is not valuable and adds very little to my life?
- Finally, write a reverse bucket list. What is it I hope I never become or do?

Living your life on purpose doesn't mean you become a calendar-toting, organizational guru. You may very well be that type, and I admire you for it. However, if you aren't uber task-oriented, I hope this chapter has helped you see how defining your purpose can still enrich your life and bless you going forward. I want you to love being you.

I spent a few of my elementary years being bullied in school. As a result, I didn't always value my own talents and uniqueness. It took me years into my adult life to appreciate and enjoy being me.

None of us is more important than anyone else. That said, we each have something specifically special about us. I have come to delight in being me – at home in my own skin – and that is one of my deepest desires for you as you slow down. I guess you could call it contentment, even though it feels so much richer than that word lets on.

A Bigger Purpose

Finally, no chapter on purpose would be complete without us looking to God. You were formed for a purpose. Your life isn't an accident. There has never been another person like you in all of history and there never will be a duplicate in all of eternity.

You may struggle to discern your purpose. That's okay. It will take most of us time to truly discover our calling. Know this: God knows what He put in you, and He isn't at a loss as to how to draw that goodness out.

Sometimes we lose sight of the intimate and personal care of God. Recently, our family went through some trying times. I knew God was in the thick of it with me. I could sense He was providing for my needs and caring for my hurts.

What I didn't expect was His dramatic intervention in our circumstances. I figured the footwork was up to me. One morning after I had ended a phone call with a friend during which we had prayed together over our family's situation, I got busy on the internet hunting down resources as if everything depended upon me. Just then, the phone unexpectedly rang.

God stepped in and changed the course of how things would go in a matter of minutes. As I hung up, I realized how little credit I had given God with regards to His omnipotent capacity to intervene.

Maybe you relate. We can feel like the person in the driver's seat. Truly, we are the copilot. I want to encourage you to invite God into the plan for your life. He has thoughts and a vantage point you don't. To leave Him out of your process is to plan in vain. God won't always say, "Go be a pet food taster!" (Yes, that job exists.) More than likely, He will guide you more subtly, leave options open for you, and open or shut doors as you move forward. The point isn't to get a written definition of your specific purpose from God, but to seek Him as you refine your vision and mission.

Make This Chapter Mine

After reading this chapter, what stands out that I want to remember?

If I had to write out a rough draft of my purpose statement today, what would it be?

What insight did I get from looking at my "not for me" list?

Who are the people I could ask to help me clarify my gifts and calling?

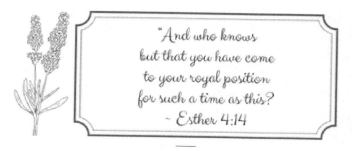

"And who knows
but that you have come
to your royal position
for such a time as this?
~ Esther 4:14

"Sometimes when you're
overwhelmed by a situation –
when you're in the darkest of darkness –
that's when your priorities are reordered."
~ Phoebe Snow

Chapter Nine

Something's Gotta Give

When I come home from the grocery, my boys usually rush into the garage to help unload the car. While I haven't emblazoned all the habits I'd like into their lives, this is one I'm grateful they've adopted.

It never fails. They grab more bags than are humanly possible to carry. I hold my breath hoping all our purchases make it from garage to kitchen counter without a major mishap. Overloading themselves feels somehow like a confirmation of their amazing capacity and future manliness.

As for me, it only took one trip a few years back where I loaded up with one too many paper bags full of our week's food to teach me the

———

hard lesson of overestimating my capacity. The handle gave way. I had no free hand to grasp the sack. (Why do catastrophes seem to click by in slow motion, single-frame?) I helplessly watched as the bag hit the ground and a jar of spaghetti sauce exploded on the carpet. Even if we manage overloading ourselves at times, eventually something's got to give, and usually a hot mess ensues.

We can't do it all.

If you are carrying too much, you know it. Like me, you've had weeks when looking at your schedule and to-do list made you want to promptly retreat to bed, pull the covers over your head, and take up an alias so no one could locate you.

I will tell you something has changed for me. I'm not sure when it happened, but as I step back and look at my life in retrospect, I see a vast difference between how I handle multiple demands now as compared to how I would suffocate and become inwardly anxious (and often outwardly impatient or irritable with those who meant most to me as a result).

In the second half of this book I'm going to lay

out a myriad of tools and mindset changes to help you live a less stressed life. For now, I simply want you to become fully aware of the level of overwhelm you are experiencing, whether it is sporadic or constant. I understand how uncomfortable this can be. I also know we won't make any lasting change until we fully acknowledge the parts of life that aren't working.

A Full Plate

My friend Christine and I were walking down a street one afternoon in Santa Barbara. We decided to meet up the day prior to a commitment we shared. Since she lives two hours away from me, we maintain our long-distance friendship through phone calls, texts, and purposeful getaways.

This day together was a rare treat. We both had a week full of demands and stressors. There were meetings and events on both our calendars requiring preparation, delegation, follow up, and oversight. I was speaking at a graduation, traveling to LA for work, and writing this book. She was attending two graduations as a part of her role in administration at her school. She also had numerous end of the year commitments.

As we walked along this lovely street lined with shops and specialty restaurants, Christine confided, "There's just so much on my plate right now." She was right, her schedule for this season was chock-a-block full. My heart longed to share with her a perspective shift.

I looked at Christine and said, "This is your plate right now," as I moved my hands out gesturing at the place we stood in that moment. Our computers were tucked away in our hotel room. The events and commitments looming in our minds belonged to the future. Responding to emails and voice messages would happen later. We were merely two friends together on a sidewalk in a beach town.

The lesson I had been learning in that season was to slow down and be fully present in the day at hand. When we start by choosing what we will and won't do, and then filter choices through our purpose and priorities, we can work in what's needed to prepare for all our commitments. That leaves enough margin to complete the essential tasks and obligations.

This approach enables us to let go of the past and future so we can be truly present.

If your plate feels full, a few changes will help you greatly. I often say, "Sometimes it's not the load we carry, but how we are carrying it that makes all the difference."

It may not be too many activities or commitments in your case. Maybe your stress comes from mentally carrying your future into your present in the form of worry or compulsive planning. Perhaps your sense of overwhelm comes from dwelling in the past, reliving hurt and loss. In Chapter Twenty-Four I'm going to share very specifically three things I have practiced to increase my ability to stay in the day at hand.

Maximum Capacity

Have you ever noticed in restaurants and movie theaters the little sign on one of the walls that says "Room Capacity"? It's always some random number like 143 people. Minds like mine wonder, what will happen if that 144th person comes into this place? Will we all self-combust from body heat? I digress.

Like the Elks' Lodge banquet room, we all have capacity. Knowing your limits will help you keep from loading up with more than you can bear.

Each person's capabilities and limits are determined by a variety of factors. Our life experiences, financial resources, personalities, talents, relationships, physical health, and season of life all contribute to how much we can or should do.

We do not have unlimited resources or unlimited options. Because of this, we must learn to budget and choose well. I don't want to facilitate a scarcity mindset here. Instead, I want us to really grasp that we can't do everything. Can you take a moment to think about your capacity?

You might feel you "should" carry more than you actually can. I want to help you get rid of that line of thinking right here. My car is a seven-seater. That's that. I shouldn't cram nine soccer team members into the seats. That would be dangerous and foolish. A healthy approach is to know both our limits and our capacity and then to go about living fully within those.

Let's be rid of "should" asap. Replace thoughts

of "should" with the word "able." Ask yourself: "What am I able to do?" instead of thinking, "I should ..." You will be amazed at how many natural limits become crystal clear with this simple shift.

Life happens. Some stages of motherhood require all we have to give and then some. We need to consider our changing capacity during different seasons of life. I'm wondering how you make adjustments for the extra demands you face, for example when you have a new baby, take up blogging, or add one more extracurricular activity into the family schedule.

Life can't just pedal along as usual when new circumstances and commitments enter the scene. Each change brings additional needs for us to accommodate. Just as you pack a suitcase for a trip, there comes a point where the bag is full. To cram it only risks it bursting at the seams. At some point, the luggage won't even close. You must adjust and take something out to make room for what is most important for your trip. Pack well for this trip, friend.

When Crisis Hits

Beyond our natural limitations, each family will

live through times of crisis. I wish this weren't so. When trauma or tragedy hits our home, we need to dial down all the expectations. It's important to have two things in place. The first is a "crisis mode" level of what you will do with your time.

When you are grieving or when you are serving your family or others in deep need, your energy level usually isn't optimal. You may need more sleep, but sometimes sleep is hard to come by. You may not be able to cook meals as elaborately or regularly as you normally do. What can you do to give yourself ten gallons of grace during these times? How can you rally the support you need?

I know it can be hard to ask for help. The process humbles us. You may feel like you should be able to do more than you are actually able. Again, with that word "should," let's ditch it. Please step back and ask yourself this question: What would I tell my good friend to do if she were going through the circumstances we are enduring right now? Often we give others so much more latitude and freedom to be human than we allow ourselves.

The second thing you need when you are going through crisis is an after-plan. How will you ease back into your intentional lifestyle when the dust settles and you are able to function more fully? You don't want to lose all you have gained. What do you need to ensure you get back to your goals and dreams?

Would accountability help? Perhaps writing some notes in your journal, or making a print out of what life looked like when you were living in less stress would give you a road map back to your pre-crisis thriving. Prepare your after-plan and know you will get to it in due time. In the meantime, if you are in crisis or trauma, let yourself off the hook and scale back to allow yourself to get through the trial.

Make This Chapter Mine

After reading this chapter, what stands out that I want to remember?

What kinds of thoughts do I have about my own capacity, and how can I live within my limits?

What tempts me to take on more than I am able?

How can I be rid of "should" as a motivator?

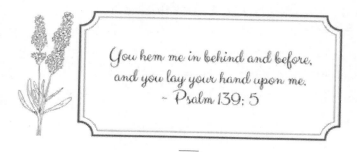

You hem me in behind and before,
and you lay your hand upon me.
~ Psalm 139: 5

"The challenge is not to manage time,
but manage ourselves.
The key is not to prioritize what's on your schedule,
but to schedule your priorities."
~ Stephen Covey

Chapter Ten

Telling Your Time Where to Go

Everyone's week contains 168 hours. Whether you are the President of the United States or the janitor at a local high school, you receive the same number of hours to spend. If you sleep seven to eight hours a night (I'm hoping you will if you don't already), you are left with approximately 115 spendable hours a week.

Years ago I started a practicing a habit called time surveying. Simply put, I log where my time is going. During my first attempts at determining what kept me busy, I quickly discovered my obligations required more time than I had in a week. How was that even possible? No wonder I was weary and chasing my tail!

What's filling your time?

You might be well aware that something has to give. The question is, what? Looking around at your life, would you cut making meals for your family? Changing diapers? Unfortunately, no. Maybe your children are older. Do you refrain from extracurriculars or playdates? These things often enrich your life and bless your children. How do you know what to release and what to keep?

To start reclaiming our time, we first need to analyze how we are spending or squandering it. We can't fix a problem until we've assessed it. It's critical to get an accurate view of what isn't working in order to apply workable solutions. You wouldn't call your doctor and allow him to prescribe a remedy without diagnosing you first.

I want you to take a time survey. You can do this one of three ways depending on what fits your lifestyle and personality best:

1) Use the form I put together for you. It's basically a blank weekly schedule. You can download it at **https://patthscott.com/slowdownmama/**.

Pick a week and log every activity in each time slot. Want to do this on steroids? Carry the blank schedule around with you for seven days. Don't change what you do, just note it all on the schedule. At the end of the week you will have an accurate snapshot of where your time goes.

2) Start by writing out your plan for the day. Then note your involvements and distractions throughout the day as you go. Keep a notebook or jot them in an app like Evernote. At the end of the day, compare your plan with your actual life. You can see what distracted you and whether your estimated time use was accurate.

3) Put two columns on a piece of paper. On one side, make a list of all your regular commitments in a typical week. In the second column note how much time you put into each one. Be sure to account for the preparation, follow up, and travel time each one consumes as well. This method is least specific, but still will give you some insight as to where your time is going. I always find it interesting to think

about how much time any activity really takes when all the facets associated with it are taken into account.

The first benefit of getting an objective look at your average week will be clearly discovering what's gobbling up your hours. Sometimes this awareness alone can spur you to choose what you want to keep or toss from your routine.

We talked about purpose in Chapter Eight. If you want to get a jump on being more intentional (which leads to a slower-paced and more content lifestyle), use your time survey to evaluate how many of your commitments and tasks line up with your purpose, dreams, and calling.

Of course, cleaning cat throw up off my sofa isn't a part of my stated life purpose. We all have mundane (and even gross) tasks and responsibilities demanding a portion of our time. We can learn to incorporate those in ways that leave room for what matters most.

Choosing What Goes

Our family purposely chose to limit team sports.

While many families commit to sports and work their lives around the time commitments needed, we had decided early on not to take on any sport in a way that would keep us traveling or require more than one night a week and a few hours each Saturday.

That was until Tae Kwon Do. Our neighbors have four boys. They invited my sons to the "bring a friend night" at their local martial arts studio. My boys came home begging to join. We capitulated and within weeks purchased the outfits and found ourselves carpooling five days a week to the Dojo.

Tae Kwon Do happened to be at 6:30pm. You can't really eat a big meal before jumping around and kicking, so we would provide the boys a light snack. Getting out at 7:30pm meant coming home ravenous and energized at 7:50pm. Suppertime and bedtime were routinely thrown off.

We lived like this for almost a year. Our boys literally loved Tae Kwon Do. It was a sacrifice, but one we willingly made. Throughout this year my heart yearned for the lost time around the table. We only ate a real family supper about twice a week. It felt like our anchor had given way.

One Sunday our pastor emphasized the point that the family supper needed to be guarded. My husband and I talked afterward and decided Tae Kwon Do had to go.

We made the announcement to the boys, telling them we loved Tae Kwon Do, but we cherish the time we share as a family more. We had to make a hard choice. We offered them the option of choosing a different extracurricular activity that would not conflict as greatly with our family time.

Though this decision was hard, we knew right away it was best. We regained our time together around the table, checking in with one another at the end of our days, and even playing board games after supper several nights a week.

Knowing our purpose and highest priorities helped us say no to something good to reclaim something even better. You can do this too. As you look through your purpose, and at other values we'll discuss in just a bit, decide what you'll remove from your routine in order to add in what aligns best with your priorities.

Make This Chapter Mine

After reading this chapter, what stands out that I want to remember?

What method of time sampling will I try?

What activities and tasks might I need to modify or cut?

What step will I take this week to lighten my load? What support do I need?

Be very careful, then, how you live—
not as unwise but as wise,
making the most of every opportunity,
because the days are evil.
Ephesians 5:15-16

*"And when they raised their eyes,
they saw no one, but Jesus only."*
~ Matthew 17:8

Chapter Eleven

Do You Mind?

Some experts have said we are living in the age of distraction. I've read competing thoughts as to whether we are actually more distracted than ever before. Let's not debate that here. The point is we are a preoccupied generation. We flit from one post to the next in our social media feeds. We scroll channels to find shows. We take on more than we can handle until our lives resemble a game of Whack-a-Mole.

I have lived through the advent of the pager (I know, I know!) and the early, prestigious, yet clunky, car telephone. I've experienced the evolution of the cell phone. I can safely say we have more capacity to distract ourselves and one another than ever before.

When I was younger, if you wanted to get

someone's attention, you called or sent them a letter, or did this other old-fashioned thing called "popping by." Now, we merely need to text, email, or leave a voice message. We can use Facetime and share files remotely. Got a problem? There's an app for that. All this access is amazing. It also magnifies the potential for distraction exponentially.

Time Suckers

As I thought about distractions and their impact on our lives, a term came to mind: *time suckers*. Distractions are like little vacuums that rob us of our opportunities to rest and be refreshed.

I sort time suckers into two groups. The first are the more obvious, external distractions. These can be things like watching TV at night, spending too much time on social media, shopping online, or other mindless activities which don't really add to our overall well-being.

Any of these in moderation can be a blessing in our life, but when we allow them to take over more than their fair share, we are robbed of the very time that would give us a peaceful heart and a sense that there is enough to go around. I'll tell you about the second set of time suckers in the next chapter.

Let's look at some common external time suckers. I want you to think about which ones you allow to pull you from the things you really want to be doing.

If you are brave enough, ask yourself why they creep in and why you don't time limit or restrict them. Often far more meaningful options are just beyond our grasp. As we identify our time suckers, we can contain them and make room for more life-giving activities and relationships.

Bright, Shiny Objects

Most of us could identify our external distractions with ease. Social media (and I enjoy it as much as you) certainly tops the charts in its ability to send us down rabbit trails and suck time away from the rest of what we intend to do with our life.

For the sake of keeping things straightforward, let's lump all the time we spend using screens into the same category. Whether we start by answering texts, checking email, reading blog posts, or searching for hotels to book for our next vacation, time seems to disappear when we engage with screens.

We will spend Chapter Thirteen talking about ways to manage and eliminate the distraction of screens. Please don't start sweating. Remember, this is about you making room for what matters most to you.

The Myth of Multitasking

We may have been sold a bill of goods when multitasking became popular. The idea is that we can do more than one thing at a time, thereby appeasing the god of productivity. Listen to this:

> *While it may seem like multitasking would be a good thing, research has shown that people who are multitasking are not doing two things at the same time. Instead, they are switching back and forth quickly between tasks. The result of this movement is that performance suffers on both tasks, and people who are multitasking are less likely to remember information later.*[1]

While I can surely throw in a load of laundry, pop some ingredients in the crock pot, and sit down to a rousing game of Catan with the boys, this really isn't multitasking. My crock pot is doing my cooking while my laundry machine cleans my clothes. I acted in sequence to get all these things to occur simultaneously. Any mom who has ever tried to help her son with a math problem while also attempting to carry on a conversation with a friend on the phone knows multitasking would be an amazing superpower, but it's not truly realistic.

In reality, when we attempt to multitask our brain toggles between tasks. Picture yourself cooking eggs in one skillet, rolling out cinnamon roll dough on the opposite counter, and slicing fruit. You have to neglect one thing while you attend to another. All that stopping and starting is exhausting. Plus, unless you are on *Master Chef*, you may burn the eggs, slice something other than fruit, and end up with undercooked, lopsided cinnamon rolls.

We do much better to take on one task at a time and follow it all the way to completion. For the record, undivided attention is far more effective than multitasking. It also gives you the satisfaction of having completed something.

As a matter of fact, *Psychology Today* noted, "Neuroscientists have known for years that dopamine is linked to positive behavior reinforcement and the 'ding, ding, ding' jackpot feeling you get when you accomplish a goal."[2] That means every time you check off a task, a little endorphin is released. These hormones give you a burst of comfort and pleasure.

That said, motherhood, by definition, often requires accomplishing a multitude of tasks simultaneously. We rarely have the luxury of focusing on one thing, especially during the toddler through early elementary years. Knowing what we do about the way our brains are wired, let's do our best to take on the fewest number of mentally demanding tasks concurrently as possible.

Tyranny of Their Urgent

Another broad category of distractions comes from the "interruptions" and urgent requests of others. If someone emails and asks me to bake cookies for the reception after my son's play, that is not a distraction. If they text me the day before the gathering, telling me the moms who were supposed to bring refreshments both have sick kids and now I am needed to pitch in both to bake last minute and give out tickets at will-call, that's a distraction. The urgency of this need tends to demand I drop all things, put on my apron, and get hopping.

I'm not saying we can't adjust our plans to meet the needs of others. Not at all. We are called to a life of love and service. However, if a pattern of dropping one thing to address another characterizes our days, we will end up feeling dominated by distraction rather than calmly fulfilling our purpose and original obligations.

Mom, Look!

Anything that diverts our attention from the task at hand can be distracting. When I talked to moms about what distracts them throughout their day, many of them simply said, "The noise!" You know what I'm talking about. Even mothers of only children can relate to the volume of sound in the home when children are present.

It can be very challenging to focus on tasks that require brain power or heart concentration (like Bible Study) when a child is marching through the living room wearing a pair of flippers belting out the soundtrack from *Little Mermaid*. I'm just sayin'.

The messes children often leave in the wake of their fun pull at us as well. For some of us, this constant state of upheaval creates an environment where concentration waxes and wanes.

While our children are a delight and a blessing, they also often demand our attention – now! Their cries for us to come quickly or help them with something often cause us to set aside our agenda.

I truly believe this distraction is one of the few we ought to ponder and usually allow. While we need to have some lines around when we are not to be disturbed as moms, we also need to cherish and preserve the occasions our children ask us to attend to them. As the mom of a teenager, I look back at the moments I set everything down with no regret. I will always wish I had practiced undivided presence even more.

Managing Distractions

I want to share a few things you can do to work

around distractions. God knows we won't eliminate them any time soon. In general, you need to initially assess the distraction. Pause when someone texts you, a bell goes off for a notification on your phone, or a person sends you a request to get something done.

Ask yourself the following questions:
First, is this life threatening? You laugh, but seriously, don't we often act as though we are faced with life and death issues when we really have much more leverage and freedom of choice? So, as I tell my kids, "If your head is still attached and nothing is on fire, carry on." Bottom line, you need to know how truly urgent the request or interruption is. Don't stop your flow for minutia.

Secondly, you want to ask if it can wait. In part of my non-writing work life, I consult with managers at a company where they oversee a number of job sites. Staff members text and call them constantly. These managers have their own workloads as well as the job of supervising people. I have helped them sort through whether to respond to interruption by asking this one question: "Can it wait?"

As moms, this same approach applies. We need

to assess the immediacy of the need being represented. A simple question as to whether something can wait will allow you to determine whether to act or to guard your time for something more important.

The third question to ask is, "Must this be done by me?" This can be a tricky one because we often feel we are the most efficient person and we know we can do things well. If you were raised like me, you may have a complex about "being the one." We fear passing tasks to others because someone might mess up.

Our reputation and concern about what others will think of us often drives us to say yes to distracting demands when the healthy answer would be no. When we set aside the opinions of others and release the outcome of the task, we can save ourselves a lot of unneeded overextension.

Make This Chapter Mine

After reading this chapter, what stands out that I want to remember?

What most frequently drags me away from important relationships and tasks?

How will I remember to ask myself if tasks can wait or be done by someone else?

How do I respond to my children when they interrupt me? Do I need to change something?

Let your eyes look directly ahead
And let your gaze be fixed
straight in front of you.
~ Proverbs 4:25

"What worries you, masters you."
~ Haddon W. Robinson

Chapter Twelve

Distracted on the Inside

The second, and sometimes more challenging, distractions we face come from inside our own minds. The internal ways we manage stress often interfere with our ability to focus and remain present. Identifying these distractions and learning new ways of coping often frees up much wasted time while giving us the sense of overall peace we have longed to obtain.

Behind the Scenes

I would venture to say internal distractions are more subtle and often more powerful than what goes on outside us. Sometimes physical needs such as hunger, fatigue, or illness can make us prone to shorter attention spans. Even more debilitating can be distracting thought patterns related to stress, worry, perfectionism, and daydreaming.

Let's quickly talk about each of these internal distractions and how they interfere with our serenity, the ability to focus on tasks, and most importantly our capacity to be fully present with people we love.

Too Stressed to be Blessed

According to the Mayo Clinic, the effects of stress on our mood include anxiety, restlessness, a lack of motivation or focus, feeling overwhelmed, irritability, anger, sadness, or depression.[1] Isn't that just a fun list of bonuses? When we experience more stress than we can handle, our focus goes out the window. We may find ourselves flitting from task to task, yet getting little done. Our interactions with our family are not the ones we want to post on Facebook and Instagram unless we are willing to add the caption: If Mama ain't happy, ain't nobody happy!

Let's look at some of God's wisdom about stress management. In the book of James, the brother of Jesus tells us to consider it all joy when we go through trials.[2] Hidden within this admonishment is a nugget of sheer gold.

When we view our trials as light and momentary,

we see them as weighed out over the course of eternity. In the moment, our circumstances can feel overwhelming. When we step back and ask how important this will be in a week, a year, or the rest of time, we obtain perspective. We still feel all the feelings, yet we are comforted by the truth that these difficulties will pass.

Wringing Our Hands in Worry

Worry may be the biggest barrier to living in the moment. Nothing wastes time like worry. While life is present in front of us and all around us, we are only half present when our minds are taken up with concerns about what will be. Often these fearful ideas fixate on the future. We imagine the worst, and as my dear friend Jessica is fond of saying, "When we worry, we never imagine God active in that future moment."

I fell in love with a Spanish proverb when I first heard it in the movie *Strictly Ballroom*. The saying goes "A life lived in fear is a life half lived."[3] I don't know about you, but I don't want a half-life. I want to live the whole life I have been given. In order to do that, I must learn to release fear and replace it with healthy trust.

This is an ongoing process. We are always growing towards increased trust and release.

Jesus reveals that the opposite of worry is living in the day at hand. He tells us not to worry, and then He immediately reminds us that our Loving Father knows all our needs.[4] Worry can be translated as the fear I won't have what I need when I need it. When we focus on God's love and provision in this given day, our worry diminishes.

Do It Just Right

We talked about perfectionism earlier. Let's look at how it distracts us from what matters most. Not only does perfectionism confine our creativity, but when we strive for perfect, we become distracted by our need to get everything just so. This can keep us inwardly preoccupied with minute details rather than freed up to try outside the box options.

Often those of us with perfectionistic tendencies end up in analysis paralysis. We can't move forward because we are stuck refining our work for the hundredth time. Bringing expectations to their right size and allowing results to be "good enough" frees our brain from the time sucker of perfectionism.

I Like Dreaming

My husband is a classic daydreamer. He works hard and may be one of the most faithful employees at his company. Still, he managed for years to fit in a totally private thought life filled with ideas about what he could have done in the past or would do in the future. While this can be a lovely way to explore and might lead to setting better goals in the future, as an isolated activity, daydreaming takes us out of the moment and keeps us from focusing on what needs to be done. The fallout often is a pile of unfinished work which can lead to increased stress.

If you are a daydreamer, I already love you. In order to spare yourself the aftermath of your imaginary jaunts to lands unseen, I suggest you allocate times of the week to let your mind wander. Make these times when you don't have obligations to fulfill and people waiting for you to come through on something important.

Since this is the only place in the book I am going to talk about daydreaming, I want to say one more thing here. Daydreamers can use their flights into fantasy as a way to numb the pain of life as is. It is often far easier to imagine what could have happened than it is to set your mind to doing something to change your circumstances.

If you are prone to a creative thought life, watch for these downsides. Use the gift of your imagination to spur yourself forward into possibility. Share your dreams with trustworthy friends and your partner. Allow them to cheer for you as you try new things.

Allow Redirection Not Distraction

While we need to be cautious about allowing distractions to change our course, we also have to remember that God often detours our plans. Have a sensitivity to divine appointments disguised as "interruptions." It is simple enough to pause and ask God whether an opportunity or request is from Him or not. Don't become so staunch in defending your time that you leave no room for Him to call you away to something you hadn't intended.

Make This Chapter Mine

After reading this chapter, what stands out that I want to remember?

What are my most frequent internal distractions (stress, worry, perfectionism, daydreaming)?

What can I do to manage these?

Is there someone I need to ask to support me as I overcome my internal distractions?

Trust in the Lord with all your heart and lean not on your own understanding; In all your ways submit to Him, and He will make your paths straight.
~ Proverbs 3: 5-6

"The more ways we have to connect, the more so many of us seem desperate to unplug."

~ Pico Iyer

Chapter Thirteen
Screen Your Time

No book on intentional living would be complete without a chapter on screens. Nothing can suck our time into a mysterious black hole like technology. Do you remember how time passed in years in Narnia while only passing hours of real time in England? Screen use is like that.

We turn on the computer or phone for one innocent little thing and before we know it, time has zipped by in our real life. Screens are good. Mismanaged, they can rob us of the intentional life we desire to build.

Let me start by assuring you of two things. One is that I appreciate my computer and cell phone so very much. I enjoy doing a Zumba workout on the X-box and being able to ask Siri to solve math problems for me. I'm not anti-tech.

I'm also not going to prescribe to you what configuration or parameters you need to set for yourself and your family around technology. Instead, I want to share some things I've learned about screen use. Then, I want to help you by providing some strategies for deciding your own limits and guidelines. You get to choose what works for you and your people.

Let's examine the time we spend on screens through the lens of motherhood. My family has had a steep learning curve in this age of technology as to how subtly a dependence can develop. In various seasons, screens have become too central in our lives. We've had to learn the hard way how easy it is to access images and content we don't want entering our children's eyes and brains.

Look in the Mirror

When it comes to choosing a healthy parameter for screen use, it's always best as parents to take a good long look at ourselves – far more uncomfortable, I know, but needed. After all, more is caught than taught, and our children are going to innately follow our example over our words.

My computer plays an integral role in my work life. I'm a writer, so I compose my books and articles on a screen. I use my phone to encourage friends and to connect with loved ones who live in other cities and states. I also use it as a map, a guide to the best restaurants, and a way to listen to podcasts when I'm on the elliptical. I get on the phone to order groceries online and to provide our choice of tunes when we rock out in the car.

Despite all that technological involvement, it is easy – from my side of the screen – to feel I am present and accessible to the people around me. My life doesn't seem separated or overly screen-involved.

Let's look at this from my child's point of view. Have you ever heard these words: "Mom, Mom, look, Mom, look!" Or, "Mom, put down your phone." Yikes. I have. Sometimes I'm "engaged" with a chat or focused on forming just the right words for a book or article. My child wants me. I feel like I'm "with" someone else. It can be so easy to put my child off in order to keep doing what I'm doing on the screen.

Occasionally this may be needed. As a way of

life, it ends up sending the message to my child: *you are not as important as this computer or phone. I don't have time for you. You are an interruption rather than a precious priority.*

The whole premise of Rachel Macy Stafford's book *Hands Free Mama* is to share her experience of letting go of distractions like technology so she could be more present with her girls. If you haven't read her book, it is heart-felt and inspiring. She is one among many moms who have become aware that we are missing some of the most priceless moments by allowing screens to substitute for in-person connection.

How to Set Your Own Limits

I want to share with you a few changes I have personally made to slow down and keep screens in their proper place in my life. I removed all games from my phone. Again, this is something I chose. When I look at my priorities and purpose in life, nothing came to the forefront that included reaching level 136 on Soda Crush or being the reigning champion of Words With Friends.

I had different times in my life when I would

"veg out" with a game for about a half hour or so. It's not toxic. Still, I'd rather play a board game with my child, draw a sketch, or spend time chatting with a friend. For me it was way too easy to default to pulling out my phone to play Bubble Witch Saga over doing something more aligned to my deepest longings. So, no games. The exception to this is the occasional game of Minecraft with my nine year old. If he invites me, I usually make time for it.

Another discipline I've adopted is setting time limits. How this works for me is that I put a little post-it note on my screen or next to me when I get on social media. The note might say something like: "Make live video for Intentional Motherhood Community; Check messages; Make a post about weekend at the coast." Yes. I get that specific. Then I set a timer. Usually I allot 20 minutes or less.

When I log on, I go through my intended tasks first. If I have some time left, I can cruise around checking my feed. When the timer goes off, I exit. This keeps me on track and makes my time on social media effective and appropriate.

On other occasions, I allow myself more time for

"frittering" and connecting with others online. I choose this instead of some other mindless recreation. Some people watch TV. I get on social media. Even then, I don't leave the time open-ended. It's too easy to allow the screen to dominate my life.

Fast to Slow

The last discipline is the hardest and most beneficial. (Why are the most profitable things often the most difficult?). Whenever I sense that social media is becoming too disproportionate or dominant in my life, I fast from it. Yep. I simply get off social media altogether. This could last anywhere from a three-day to a six-week stretch. I delete the app from my phone to eliminate temptation. For longer periods of time, I ask people I trust to lead my Intentional Motherhood Group for me while I'm gone.

Fasting of any kind is challenging. What usually happens the first few days is my mind wanders and I want to take pictures of my coffee or the passage in my devotional to post and share online. (Yes, I'm that sick.) My son says something adorable and a post might form in my head. This is a tell-tale sign that I for sure needed a break. When that urge hits, I mentally share my "post" with God and those around me instead, or I simply treasure it in my heart.

Over time I become less drawn to what I would have posted and I don't notice what I'm missing. Nature abhors a vacuum – so does my nine year old, but that's not relevant here. Where we leave space, something will come in to fill the vacancy. In the case of a screen fast, I have more time to devote to projects like my writing. I can delight in hobbies like drawing or gardening.

My presence disengages from behind a computer, and I am available to my family in more complete ways. I always return to Facebook and Instagram because social media is not all bad. Not at all. I simply need to recalibrate so I can participate in healthy moderation. A fast reorders my priorities and restores my self-control.

Family Screen Use

Once you have screens under control in your own life – or as you progress in this – you need to determine what screen use looks like for your family. If you are married, obviously this is a team process. In the first parenting book I coauthored, we have a whole chapter on setting screen limits.

Let's keep it simple for the sake of brevity. Do some reading about screens and how they can impact developing brains. The data from science can be a rude awakening. I'm not an extremist. Well, I can be, but I work against that tendency. While some families will choose to have no TV, no X-Box, and no phones, that's not the majority of the world these days. More of us will need to figure out ways to allow screens without permitting them to take over and interfere with real connection.

Once you know what the potential downfalls of excessive or unmonitored screen use can be, set limits on time, content, and capacity. Voila, you are golden. It's simple and not always easy, I know. Some great books to help you are Kathy Koch's book *Screens and Teens* and Gary Chapman's book *Growing up Social: Raising Relational Kids in a Screen Driven World*. I also highly recommend Axis.org as they send out a weekly newsletter by email and have parent guides on social media and technology.

Boundaries with screens are needed. Allowing

our kids to consume unsupervised, unlimited media would be like sending them into a candy store and asking them to eat just a little and be sure to choose well. They simply aren't equipped to ensure their own health and safety.

Say Yes to Fun

Instead of focusing on all the "no you can't" and "turn that off" as a primary tone in the home, make sure you provide your children with a whole lot of good, old-fashioned hands-on fun. Nothing beats screens like connected time with friends and family. Every child truly prefers this. We simply need to regularly make the effort to set it up and to create an environment conducive to less screens and more creative activity.

We are blessed to live in a neighborhood where many of the families have lived here for over ten years. Our children have grown up together. We have trampolines and swimming pools in many of the backyards.

I make it a practice when my sons ask for screen time to usually make my first answer no. They used to grumble a bit, but I found nine out of ten times, after a short protest involving wandering around aimlessly or complaining of boredom, they concocted something else to do – something imaginative that didn't involve a screen.

Real Connection

The bottom line on social media, online gaming, and most other screen-based engagement is that it never substitutes for real, in-person relationships. In her book, *Breaking Busy*, (which I loved!) Alli Worthington asks this question:

"Do we find genuine connection or do we fill our time with loose connections based on acquaintances? Like everything in life, it depends on how we use it."[1]

Then she shared this result of research about social media:

> *"The more we use Facebook and other forms of social media as a passive participant, scrolling through news feeds and Instagram images, the more loneliness and sadness we feel."*[2]

Human beings were made with some basic needs. Two of the deepest of these are to feel loved and to know we belong. Social media does not provide for those. We must go beyond the screen to find real relationship. To do that we are going to have to sacrifice screen time to clear the way for the riskier, but far more fulfilling experience of building face-to-face relationships.

I'll get a little vulnerable here. Being busy and living at breakneck speed kept me from being aware of my deep longing for connection. I filled my own tank with feelings of accomplishment. That filling was only temporary and never satisfied me. I justified being unable to connect because I was so very busy. When I slowed down, not everyone around me followed suit.

I am still working on risking asking people to spend time together. I sometimes force myself to make phone calls instead of texting. Even harder, I am learning to reach out when I am lonely or hurting.

It felt comfortable to hide behind a screen. Setting technology aside to cultivate relationships hasn't been completely dreamy and wonderful. There have been times I showed up for an amazing motherhood moment only to have my children run off with friends. On other occasions, I wanted to spend time with a woman from church and she had too much on her calendar. I don't let these setbacks hinder me from continuing to prioritize people over technology.

Growth takes time, and it is hard work. Go easy on yourself as you move from busy to available. I will tell you one thing. I wouldn't trade a month of lonelier, more vulnerable days for the lifestyle I was living before I intentionally cut back. The relationships I am building and the people I am investing my heart and time into are worth the risk and all the uncomfortable emotions it takes for me to be present.

Make This Chapter Mine

After reading this chapter, what stands out that I want to remember?

How does screen time take me away from what I need or want to do?

What actions do I know I need to take to set healthy boundaries on my own screen use?

What limits do I want to set for our family?

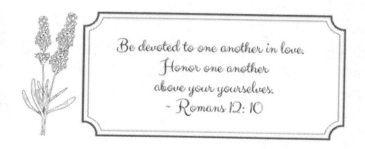

Be devoted to one another in love.
Honor one another
above your yourselves.
~ Romans 12: 10

""Never be too busy for the people you love. Never allow pursuits or possessions to become bigger priorities than your relationships."
~ Dave Willis

Chapter Fourteen
Savoring Relationships

My boys can tell you one surefire way to drive me bonkers: make me play Candyland. I'd pretty much rather stick toothpicks in my eyes and run barefoot on their bedroom floor before they pick up the Legos. Of course, I never offered that alternative – they might have taken me up on it!

I have endured the game for their sake. Still, my mind drifted as I counted down the minutes left until one of us reached the castle. Motherhood at its finest, I know. Meanwhile, my husband seems to have this unnatural ability to tolerate mindless preschool games. He has more patience in his pinky finger than I have obtained after years of walking with Jesus.

Oh, My Wandering Mind!

Along the same lines, while I don't have ADD, I used to have this part of my brain that twitched and started to go numb when my child most needed my attention for something mundane like explaining every detail of how they made their construction paper angel in Sunday School.

I meant well. I did. I would unwittingly start to phase out and get a bit antsy. The worst part is, they could tell. They tried to refocus me by saying, "Mom, Mom, are you listening?" I would strain to force my concentration as I replied, "Yes, honey, go on."

As long as we are entertaining true confessions of awful motherhood moments here, I'll tell you one more: bedtime. At the close of a long day, with my sons snugly tucked in bed, I often hit the dead end of my reserves. As you know, bedtime is the hour of great and deep thoughts for children. Being wiped out, I sometimes rushed through our routine, gave kisses, and said, "No more words, it's time for sleeping."

My overfull lifestyle left me zero energy to sit still for blow-by-blow conversations about craft projects or bedtime junior theological inquiries.

I hadn't learned to savor the moments. I missed opportunities to cherish the precious people I loved the most. It's not that I never had late night chats with my children. I simply didn't make them a priority. I needed to move on.

The Gift of Presence

As I grew in living according to my purpose, I began to practice the habit of being fully present. What that looks like is setting down my phone, computer, or whatever else I am doing and simply being with the person or people who most want my attention.

I won't lie. At first this required real discipline. I would find my mind wandering to my to-do list or another activity that more fully lined up with my agenda. When that happened, I quietly rehearsed the reminder: *this person is my agenda. I don't want to let this season of motherhood, friendship, or marriage pass me by while I'm busy mentally being somewhere else.*

Just the other day, my son was telling me about a show he had watched on TV. Let's put it this way: the show lasted 20 minutes; his description may have been just about as long. Somewhere in the middle of our time together – while he marched around the porch coffee table, picked up leaves, laughed, and expressed the story with all sorts of variations in his voice – I had a thought. I was fully with him. He was delightful. This whole moment was joy! Watching him exuberantly share this story was a gift. It wasn't lost on me, and I wasn't itching to be somewhere else.

The older my sons get, the more I realize the value of making time to spend with them. Our ways of connecting change as they mature. Thankfully neither of them is that keen on Candyland anymore!

In younger years, time together meant playing on the floor or reading aloud. Now that they are older, it might mean jumping on the trampoline or going on a scooter ride. It can also look like sitting and listening as they share about something important that happened to them or discussing ideas and plans together.

Sometimes my investment in their lives is as simple as popping popcorn for the gaggle of kids hanging at our home, then attempting to inconspicuously blend into the furnishings as I take it all in. Pausing to observe the sweetness of this season – a full house, my boys' friendships, my ability to serve them – fills my heart to overflowing. That's the fruit of slowing and savoring.

Chew Before You Swallow

As moms, we tend to learn to gulp down our food. We even eat on the run, taking pieces of our children's leftover fast food lunches and trying to sustain ourselves on this hurried consumption. Savoring involves unhurriedly letting life melt in our mouth and go down slowly.

When we commit to savoring our relationships, we will taste goodness we had been overlooking. We can learn to appreciate what is right in front of us. I want to ask you, as I often ask myself: What is slipping by unnoticed? What are you gulping down? What flavor are you completely missing? What nourishment is lacking because of your speed and inattention?

I hope you aren't giving yourself a royal guilt trip as you answer. The point is to identify what needs to change so you can move forward. Don't form yet another stick to beat yourself up for what's not working. If you feel some sadness over the way you have been living, go ahead and grieve. Then use that remorse to fuel your motivation to slow down and be present.

Three Key Types of Relationships

When my oldest was younger I came up with a way of teaching him about the three types of relationships he would need in his life using a playground slide as the example.

When you are very little, you can't quite make it up the ladder to cruise down from the top on your own. Along comes someone who has mastered the slide. They help you up the ladder or give you that final hand up from the top.

These people are your mentor friends. They have been down the road further than you, and they know they lay of the land. Mentors guide you and pour into your life. We all need them.

Now picture the slides built next to one another. You are now old enough to get up the slide, and you and your friend run up and speed down together, sometimes holding hands as you slide with one another.

These people are your side-by-side friends. In adult verbiage, I would call these reciprocal relationships. Sometimes you pour into them; equally, they support you. You go through life together. You listen to one another without passing judgement. Think of the old Bill Withers song "Lean on Me." Side by side friends become your go-to people to receive support in a crisis or to share in your celebrations.

The final type of friend is a younger child on the playground. You are now a slide master. You've got this thing down pat. You can even slide with your eyes closed, going backwards with your head aiming down. You watch this younger child struggling to get up the ladder and you remember what it was like. You give them a leg up.

You become the mentor in this ministry relationship. We all need to pour out from the places we have received. Life comes full circle as we give to others from our hard-earned experience.

Now It's Your Turn

Here's where I'm going to ask you to do a little work drawing your own lines. I want you to ask yourself who your people are. Your family is probably at the center of your life, and they rightfully get the bulk of your time and energy.

Outside your family, which relationships are you devoting yourself to cultivating? Relationships are like plants in a garden. They need care, weeding, feeding, and light to flourish. If we neglect our relationships, they will wither and ultimately die.

On the next page you will find a diagram with three concentric circles. If you would, picture yourself at the middle and then write the names of the people who matter the very most to you in the closest circle. Then in the second and third circles write the names of reciprocal friendships, mentors, and precious people to whom you minister.

Each circle has a smaller bandwidth as you get further out. That has to do with how much time you can afford to invest in these people. You simply cannot be all things to all people. You can be something amazing to your designated people. Save your best for them and make sure you live a life that prevents those in your inner circle from living on your dregs.

Now it's your turn. Take the time you need to fill in the circles:

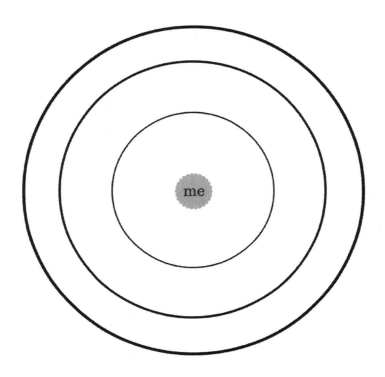

I hope visualizing your circles clarifies your "to-love" list. Now decide how you are going to be present for the people closest to the center. How much time can you give each one in a given day, week, or month. What is their love language? What ways would they like to be with you? What can you enjoy together?

Being the Friend You Long to Have

If you are drawing a blank in any of these areas,

I understand. There were years when I had drifted from certain friendships. Some friends had moved and people had gone about their lives. New connections hadn't deepened.

If that describes you, I encourage you to do what I did. I scanned the horizon and asked myself which people I would most like to have as friends. I purposed to pray for them, call regularly, and initiate connection. Some of these women have become dear friends of mine over the years. I would have missed out on treasured relationships if I had held back or stayed stuck feeling neglected and fearful.

Maybe you have noticed that people often don't initiate time together unless it is organized around an event or activity. I decided to change that in my relationships. I don't keep score as to who calls me or invites me. Instead I reach out to women who matter to my heart.

Making the Effort

Slowing down means making relationships central to your life. Whether you are an

extrovert who thrives in large social settings and finds yourself surrounded with people at every turn or an introvert with only a handful of special people and the craving to find a quiet spot by yourself on a regular basis, a fulfilling life includes cultivating meaningful connection.

This never happens by accident. Someone initiates and risks. Someone responds, which is also risky, and the connection becomes strengthened with each movement we make towards one another. Making room for relationship means determining in your heart that people matter enough to cut out what interferes with the ability to be fully present.

One of the sweet friendships I have been able to cultivate over the past few years is with a woman named Suzanne. I adore her kind and thoughtful heart. She never takes center stage, so to befriend her, you need to extend yourself to initiate connection.

As I sat back one year doing my exercise to determine the people with whom I wanted to pursue friendship, she came to mind. I reached out to tell her how much I enjoy her company and how I hoped we could spend more time together –to connect, share, and pray.

She responded with such warmth. Since then we try to have lunch or meet up as regularly as we are both able. Some seasons are harder than others with moves of homes, illnesses of parents, or needs of children, but we make the effort.

One day Suzanne invited me to her home for lunch. I walked in to see a spread on the table with plates of lettuce leaves, cooked chicken and various toppings all beautifully arranged with two place settings carefully provided. The whole scene was like a deep breath of fresh air. We sat for lunch, sharing our hearts and reveling in the sweetness of God's provision between us.

At one point the FedEx delivery gal arrived. She was so tickled to see us eating such a delightful lunch together. Times like this are glimpses of heaven on earth and we are able to have them because we have chosen to slow down and make the effort to be fully present.

What Savoring Is Not

Savoring relationships isn't all bliss and rose-colored living as we watch our children frolic in the waves at dusk on the beach. (Cue romantic Music.) Nope. Nope. Nope. (Cue loud scratch of record player.) We are going to have to allow mess, failure, delay, and loss of control.

As we pursue connection and our deepest purposes and passions, life will not flow according to plan. Slowing down to become intentional is not another formula to appease our need to be in the driver's seat. On the contrary, when we choose to invest in people, we dive into the uncertain and the everyday ordinary. This is not the stuff of Hollywood movies.

Learning to allow room for other people and their present needs means making space for unfinished business, uncomfortable emotions and vulnerability. This path away from micromanagement will ultimately give you the greatest joy and freedom you can know. Just to forewarn you, savoring relationship isn't a neat and tidy proposition.

Savoring also doesn't translate into being a perfect mom who rarely loses her cool and never says, "Hurry up!" to her kids when running late. We are works in progress. I still blow it. I regularly have had to sit with my boys, apologize, retie our heart strings, and start from scratch.

I've read some books on slowing down that make it seem like everyone is living on fluffy billows of clouds with not a care in the world. I don't want to leave you with the impression that we somehow live a saintly life here at the Scott home. We fall down and we get back up. We don't expect unrealistic bliss and perfection. Savoring is how we set our hearts in the direction of loving well.

Savoring vs. Responsibilities

One more thing savoring isn't. We don't sit around relishing relationships at the expense of skipping going to the grocery store, letting the laundry pile up, and avoiding paying the bills.

Each of us needs to determine how to include being present for those who matter most to us while continuing to attend to the basic duties of life. Sometimes this means doing chores together. We can ask our children to wait or occupy themselves while we finish a task. Building in the habits we will discuss in Chapter Twenty-Six will help you complete homecare while leaving margin for savoring your people.

Make This Chapter Mine

After reading this chapter, what stands out that I want to remember?

Do I have mentors, side-by-side friends, and ministry relationships?

How can I pour into the people who are central to my life?

Where do I want to invest more time or energy?

_Now that you have purified yourselves
by obeying the truth so that
you have sincere love for each other,
love one another deeply, from the heart._
~ 1 Peter 1: 22

*"Healthy boundaries are not walls.
They are the gates and fences that allow you
to enjoy the beauty of your own garden."
~ Lydia H. Hall*

Chapter Fifteen

Freedom Through Limits

When our oldest son was eight and our second-born was an infant, we often enjoyed taking a Sunday drive after church. Sometimes we drove about an hour from home to hike in nature. Other weekends the drive itself was the event.

We drove through rolling hills and ravines running between open farmland. On one particular road cattle roam freely. We found ourselves stopping the car to allow a herd to cross, and even waiting while they stood blocking our way. Basically, we were at their mercy.

Other roads had "cattle guards" installed at various points. These metal grates prevented the livestock from meandering onto the lane

could either hit them or be
from driving.

   ιis weird thing about cows. I love them.
   my obsession started as a girl when we
   arly went to the local dairy to buy milk. As
   mother made our purchases in the farm
   ɔre, I would stand on the fence waiting for a
   ιeifer to come near. The grit of their tongue as
they licked my hand and the soft gentle
expression in their eyes became part of the
fabric of precious childhood memories.

As much as I adore cattle, having them
indefinitely impede our family outing on a
Sunday drive made things a bit tricky. I wasn't
fond of this intrusion on our plans, especially
when our napping infant woke due to the car
sitting still.

The cattle guards provided a healthy separation.
Like any good boundary, both parties were
protected and life flowed more smoothly with
the limits more clearly defined.

Like the road my family travelled on our Sunday
drives, our lives need "cattle guards" to protect
us from all that might stampede or block
intentional living. Simply put, we need to

develop healthy boundaries.

Once you have a sense of purpose, have clarified your goals within it, and have filtered the details into your weekly and daily plans, you have to put up some boundaries to protect yourself. Otherwise, distractions, others' demands, and the draining impact of toxic relationships can keep you from living for what is most vital.

Healthy limits don't set themselves. You have to be diligent to set up these markers and protect yourself and what matters most. Hold fast to what you have decided is your priority. No one else will do this for you.

Don't Fence Me In

If you are a more free-spirited person, you may wince at the idea of structuring and guarding your time. Knowing your boundaries and living within your limitations will actually free you up for much more of what you want to include in your life.

Structure isn't meant to stifle or suffocate us. We don't have to live a rigid existence. Structure ensures we accomplish the things we have to do so we are able to include the things that are most important. When we aren't bogged down with others' responsibilities, unhealthy relationships, and excessive distractions, we actually have more freedom than ever.

Stay in Your Lane

Picture the lines on a freeway. They make sure everyone stays on track. When we take the time to determine what we are called to do and devote ourselves to the highest priority in our life, we know our lane. Sometimes, other people will attempt to draw us into their lane. They will put responsibilities on us that are not ours to fulfill. Knowing our lane can help us deflect those things which might keep us from doing what we are meant to do.

As a mother, I am the only person my children will call Mom. My friends have other friends. My job has other employees. Many other wonderful writers compose books to bless readers. I am the only mom my boys will have in life. The exclusivity of my role as wife and mother causes this calling to be the highest in my life. When other needs and tasks arise, I can stay in my lane – eyes ahead on my purpose, eyes upward to God for guidance.

Not every need is ours to fill. Not every job is ours to do. Not every hurt is ours to comfort. We need to know where we are meant to serve, give, and work and let the rest go. Each "yes" I give means drawing lines to say many "no" answers to what competes with that "yes." These boundaries protect my "yes" so I can focus and do it justice.

We have to stop here to talk about expectations others have of us. This can be such a sticky wicket. The more time we spend really clarifying our roles in life and the calling we feel led to fulfill, the less we will be willing to take on trivial tasks that aren't ours. People have to adjust to our boundaries. We need to set them with gentleness and respect. Still, people may try to shame or cajole us into bending. Standing firm with our boundaries takes practice. It gets easier over time.

Knowing my calling and staying in my lane doesn't mean I won't pick up chairs after a church event or print my friend's flyers on my color printer because those tasks don't line up with my calling to write and minister to women.

I'm still able to use my margin to bless people in many ways. The point is I don't get derailed and sidetracked as easily when I set boundaries to protect what matters most.

If you keep thinking you want to be clearer about your purpose, you can revisit Chapter Eight. I also highly recommend the book *Essentialism* by Greg McKeown. His message is life changing.

Boundaries as Protection

Have you ever been in a toxic relationship? I'm talking about a connection with a friend or family member who gets jealous, is dominant or manipulative, or who tilts the relationship in their favor and takes advantage of you.

Toxic relationships drain our time and energy. Not only do we spend ourselves on these people with little good coming from our investment, but our resources are zapped after we leave their presence. We feel depleted for hours or days after an interaction with a toxic person.

You can easily see why setting boundaries in relationships is so critical. Even in healthier relationships, knowing where we stop and the other person starts provides the foundation for healthy interactions.

I've been in several toxic relationships in the past. In a particular friendship I allowed the person to treat me as less than and send subtle messages of shame and rejection my way. I spent effort proving my worth to that person and then would reel emotionally after being with them for any extended period of time.

The relationship didn't start on unhealthy terms, but over time it eroded until I was knee deep in toxic mire. I had to extricate myself, set clear limits, and put a lot of space between us. In my mind I determined acceptable parameters for being with this person (in large groups for time-limited activities) and avoided circumstances that were unhealthy (being alone or spending indefinite amounts of time together).

In *Breaking Busy*, Alli Worthington says,

> *Keeping true connections in your life and not allowing negative people to drain you dry will help you break busy. You will be spending your precious time on your most important relationships, those that fill you up instead of draining the life out of you.*[1]

Blurred Lines

With the advent of the internet, and so much online capacity to accomplish work and connect with others, our boundaries have become blurred. We no longer have a separation between work and home, or friendship, business, and ministry. We have to be more intentional about carving out time and putting parameters around those aspects of our lives to keep them sacred and safe.

To counterbalance the intrusion of the internet, we need to carve out designated times for special people. Our screen use has to be purposefully limited. For people like me who work from home, we need to clearly define times and places for work and then set all business aside so we can be present for home life.

I picture the protective boundaries I set around time with precious people and vital activities as being like a police tape at a crime scene or the laser beams guarding the Crown Jewels. These markers tell everyone the other side of this line is important and only to be crossed by authorized people in designated ways.

God's Boundaries for Us

Sometimes God sets a limit on us, as any good parent will do. As parents, we have bedtime rules for our children so they will benefit from the optimal amount of sleep. Likewise, God sets limits for our wellbeing.

Many years ago I heard Charles Swindoll speak of the four answers God gives to our prayers. They were "go," "no," "grow," and "slow." Go means yes. This is when God agrees with our request and gives us what we have asked of Him. We love this answer.

"No," of course, means no. We aren't quite as fond of this answer, and sometimes we respond a bit like our children when they asked for a cookie before supper and we lovingly declined. A no answer can feel like God didn't hear us or care about our wants and feelings. As we mature, we understand a no response from God is always given in the spirit of love with the greatest care possible.

"Grow" means we have to mature to be prepared to receive the yes God has for us. This is akin to us waiting to put our child on a bicycle until they are ready and have the potential skills to learn to ride well.

"Slow" means God has to work out details within the circumstances or people involved in a coming yes answer. The answer will be yes when all the pieces fall in place as they should.

"Grow" and "slow" answers can feel like a no answer in the moment because we aren't getting what we want when we want it. God's no always prepares us for His perfect yes. As we learn to trust God increasingly, we have confidence in His timing regardless of the outcome. All of these answers provide boundaries for us which help us either move forward or stay put according to what is best for us and all people involved.

One other way God sets limits on us is through pruning. Sometimes we have to allow this cutting back to make room for greater harvest. As we walk with Jesus, we will experience regular pruning imposed upon us by God. He promises this and graciously informs us to expect it.

Just as our gardens go through seasons, our lives, ministry, work, and friendships often go through refinement at periodic intervals. I will never cease to be amazed at how surprised I am when pruning comes along. I am often so taken up with fruit that I can't imagine the cutting and thinning will occur.

God has designed pruning for healthy productivity in connection to Him. If we are to have an abundant life, we know there will be times of loss along the way. During pruning we feel exposed and bare. We can feel stagnant and lose sight of our value outside our productivity. God uses these times to bring out new growth and increased dependence upon Him. He is always preparing us for the next best thing.

Make This Chapter Mine:

After reading this chapter, what stands out that I want to remember?

How can I put healthy boundaries in place around my time?

What relationships are toxic to me? How can I draw better lines?

Do I struggle with the boundaries God has for me?

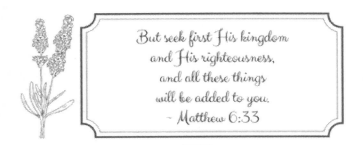

But seek first His kingdom and His righteousness, and all these things will be added to you.
~ Matthew 6:33

"Rest is a matter of wisdom, not law."
~ Woodrow Kroll

Chapter Sixteen

A Time of Rest

Let's talk about something crucial to a slow life: rest. Much like a crabby toddler, something in us resists the gift of much needed downtime.

I picture my boys. They are like chocolate and vanilla – so opposite. Once on a long drive as we were filling time, we played a little game of *Would You Rather?*. I asked questions like "lake or ocean?", "hip-hop or classical?", "sushi or pizza?", and on it went. They had opposite preferences on almost every point.

When it comes to rest, they lived out this contrast in such a noticeable way. My oldest fought naps from 20 months old on. He would throw fits that ought to have caused the neighbors to call authorities. That boy would not nap.

Along came my second-born. He actually said

things like, "Mom, I feel tired. I'm going to lie down." Um, what? Who has heard of a three year old announcing their need for sleep with such articulate self-awareness? I remember sitting in dumb silence as he took his blankie down the hall and snuggled up. I never got accustomed to this anomaly.

Riskers and Resters

I have come to believe there are two types of people when it comes to rest. Our pastor talked about this once in a sermon. He drew the analogy in terms of faith. There are riskers and resters. Riskers get busy doing things. There's a world out there in need of help, salvation, and support. Let's go!! Then there are the resters. They say, "Let's wait on God. We need to pray over this. It's wise to assess a situation before jumping in." Both these types have great things to offer the world. Riskers need the resters to pull them back a bit as they add wisdom and perspective to decisions; resters need the riskers to get them moving and put an end to analysis paralysis.

If you are a rester you may not need me to tell you to take it easy. Then again, you may. If you are a risker, though, I know you. I get it. You may think rest is for weaklings. Perhaps you've even had thoughts like, "I'll rest when I'm geriatric. Meanwhile I've got things to do. I'm not wasting my life with rest." Right?

Rest is a Gift

I'm going straight for the jugular here. God rested. Not only that, He ordained rest. Before you go telling me that is an Old Testament command which expired when Jesus came, I want you to examine some New Testament thoughts on rest.

Please leave your shame and workaholism at the door and see these verses as invitations. No loving parent puts their child down for a nap to punish them. We know a nap is the very best thing for our child. They will be refreshed and able to be their sweetest self after resting. Yes, in our humanness we long for that nap for our own sake as parents. We would pay big bucks to get them to settle on certain days. Still, our biggest reason for wanting them to nap is so they get their own need met.

That is what God is doing as He prescribes rest. He knows rest is good for us – actually one of the biggest gifts and blessings He offers. How can I say that? I have studied the Old Testament and the concepts of rest and Sabbath. God values this enough to make it one of the Ten Commandments. It has paramount importance. I'll get to that in a bit, but first let's look at some passages from the New Testament about rest.

Work at Rest

In His letter to the Hebrews, God says, "There remains, then, a Sabbath-rest for the people of God; for anyone who enters God's rest also rests from their works, just as God did from His. Let us, therefore, make every effort to enter that rest, so that no one will perish by following their example of disobedience."[1]

Let's unpack this. I get a little over-excited when I read the underlying meanings of Scripture in the Greek or Hebrew. Geeky, I know. That saying, "a Sabbath-rest," is actually a phrase that means the blessed rest from toils and troubles looked for in the age to come by the true worshippers of God.

What God is saying here is that the rest He offers us – the rest that remains with us – is a foretaste of heaven we can experience here on earth. Jesus left this rest behind for us as a gift. Remember when Jesus said, "My peace I leave you?" Yep. That's the stuff.

In the next part of this passage we are told those of us who enter God's rest also rest from our works. In this case, rest also means a safe and tranquil dwelling place where God abides. We rest from our doing, our accomplishing, our producing. We do this as God did.

We are told in Genesis God rested from all His work on the seventh day. His rest was a sign of satisfaction with all He had done. He pulled back and ceased from creating. Creating is good. Resting is also blessed.

Let me get a bit personal and ask you when the last time was you rested as God rested. Are you harping back to naptime as a toddler? If you are, soul sister, I hear you. For the first ten years of my marriage, my husband used to occasionally say, "You never sit down." How could I with so much to do? Ay yi yi.

In the last portion of this thought on Sabbath-rest, we are called to be diligent to enter that rest. What? Diligent? Isn't that working? I thought I was resting. Here's where we can see so clearly how well God knows us and our challenges. Resting takes work. We have to make effort to carve out times of rest, and we have to pursue rest in the same way we pursue work. In order to enter rest, we swim upstream against our flesh and our desire to earn credits by achieving. We are going against the grain of demands and to-dos.

God closes this passage with the caution that we need to be careful not to fail. Fail at what? What example of disobedience are we being warned not to follow? Here it is. We can be such self-sufficient, busy bees. We have to get things done – important things. This mindset finds its foundation in mistrust and fear (ouch!). We tend to rely on ourselves instead of knowing rest is possible because outcomes don't hinge on our activity, but His.

Rest is the ultimate expression of trust and humility. We can let things go and release what is done and what is left undone because our view of our self is right sized. We aren't puffed up with importance, and we aren't shrunken with fear. Instead we lean on God and find our rest in Him.

A Quiet Life

In his letter to the Thessalonians, Paul says, "Make it your ambition to lead a quiet life: You should mind your own business and work with your hands, just as we told you."[2]

A quiet life. What could that mean? I'm a wordy girl. Am I supposed to take up being a mime? Should I silence myself online and never write to bless? Beyond my own "noise," my home is anything but quiet. I mean, I'm raising boys and hosting the neighborhood most days.

I hope you are as tickled as I am at the translation of this phrase, "a quiet life." It is said of those who are not running hither and thither, but stay at home and mind their business. The opposite of a quiet life is someone who is always in other people's business.

How do we involve ourselves in others' business? Sometimes it can be through outright gossip. We might also compare and covet. Maybe you find yourself judging people around you. Hither and thither, my friend. We all do it. God is telling us there's a better, more restful way of living, and it involves concerning ourselves with the domain He's given us rather than being overly involved in other people's assignments and performance evaluations.

Another translation for that word, "quiet" is, you guessed it, rest. We need to make rest a lifestyle. God is inviting you to it. Is your current plan better than His? Mine sure isn't.

The busy, overstuffed life I was living and am continuing to outgrow was an example of my best thinking and implementation. His plan is abundant life, not one so impacted with commitment I can hardly catch a breath. Rest is integral to a healthy life in God.

The Heart of Rest

If you are ready to work rest into your life, I want to help you. Ideally you will have two levels of rest and three frequencies. Let's talk about the levels of rest first.

Rest is a lifestyle. As Tim Keller says, we work from a place of rest.[3] That inner rest – the one we come to contain within our hearts – is what we crave. It is diametrically opposite to the way we have been living as frenetically busy women. Jesus invites us to come to Him for rest.[4] Rest at its heart is communion with Jesus in abiding love.

When we practice rest frequently enough over time, we make room for God to develop a restful spirit within us. From my experience, as I have grown towards an increasing inner rest, I am less easily flapped by outward disturbance. My calm heart gives me the capacity to endure upsetting circumstances without losing my cool. If you knew me, you'd be giving God a standing ovation right about now.

Carving Out Time for Rest

This second level of rest is the practical level. This is where we put in the hours and do our "work" to carve out times of resting. It is essential to include both aspects of rest into our lives. Inner rest is often a fruit of the habit of resting.

Make This Chapter Mine

After reading this chapter, what stands out that I want to remember?

Am I a risker or a rester? What people balance me in this?

How do I view rest – as a gift, a chore, or something just out of reach?

What is the biggest barrier to my resting?

Come to Me all who are heavy-laden and are weary and I will give you rest.
~ Matthew 11:28

"Take rest; a field that has rested
gives a bountiful crop."
~ Ovid

Chapter Seventeen
Working at Rest

Let's talk about the three frequencies of rest. If you have ever traveled to Europe, especially the region around the Mediterranean, you have experienced the rhythm of their average day. Sometime after lunch there is a slowing, a siesta, or a tea time. Knowing how we are wired, these cultures have built in a daily time when work ceases and rest is intentionally provided.

As the compulsive spirit of America has influenced other cultures, we see some movement away from this wisdom. Still, in many countries an afternoon time of recharging remains alive and well.

It is so wise to build in daily times of rest. In many early Christian communities, and in the high church which traces its roots back to those, there are practices called the "daily office." There is no actual office associated with this spiritual discipline. People who practice the daily office, set aside time throughout the day to stop their work, pull back, read Scripture, pray, and sit with God.

Whether you do something formal or just curl up on the couch for a ten-minute breather, I encourage you to build in a daily rest. Yeah, yeah. No, really. You can thank me later.

Ancient Roots of Sabbath

Recently a revival has sprung up with a return to Old Testament practices among certain Christians. One of these rituals is weekly Sabbath keeping. I'm not going into the theological underpinnings of this movement. However, I do want to talk to you about the benefits of setting a whole day aside to refrain from work to give yourself a rest.

Emily P. Freeman (Ohhhh, I love that girl!) spoke about Sabbath on her podcast *The Next Right Thing*.[1] She shared thoughts from a book called *The Dusty Ones* by A.J. Swoboda. Listen to this:

Dr. Swoboda mentions that nowhere in the

Bible are we asked to create or make Sabbath. Instead, we protect it and enter into it. It's not something we make up. It's something we've been asked to take care of. He points out how the Jews knew this and they spoke of keeping Sabbath, not creating it. They would understand the difference. It isn't something they decided to do because they were really tired and needed a break. No, Sabbath is a gift, and they were wise to receive it.

Oh, yes! We receive Sabbath; we keep and protect Sabbath so we may enter into it. We don't create it or make it. Isn't that lovely?

Hi, overachiever girl. I'm talking to you. I can imagine how all this talk of Sabbath-keeping might be hitting that productive shell around your heart. Task: Sabbath-keeping. Check. You get out your calendar, grab your color-coded markers, and pick one that says "rest" to you (possibly the pink one, but not boldly pink, subtle and soothing, more like a soft salmon). Then, you proceed to mark the next 52 Sundays "Sabbath; Sabbath; Sabbath ..." Oh, girl.

Let's dial this back just a smidge. I appreciate

ambition as much as the next person. I also know from personal experience that I'm great, even perfect, at planning out amazing, show-stopping spiritual practices. I dive in with no hesitation. Then, like Peter, I'm out when the heat gets too hot in the kitchen.

What if we try this on for size instead. Could you consider looking at the coming week? Pick a day. Yep. It doesn't have to be Sunday or Saturday. It can be any day the Lord has made. Plan to rest that whole day. I don't mean stay in bed, refuse to talk to your children, and eat ice cream for breakfast, lunch, and dinner (though, you keep your Sabbath, and I'll keep mine). I am talking about refraining from the stuff you call work. Don't shop. Don't plan. Don't produce. Most of all, don't strive.

This may look a bit like a giraffe giving birth at first – awkward! That's okay. Don't give up. After your first experiment with a whole day of Sabbath, go for week two. Make note of what worked and what was a bit wonky, and then carry on. In due time, if you keep trying this out most weeks, you will get better at knowing what Sabbath-keeping means for you. There are great books on this as well. Check out Emily P.

Freeman's podcast episode 40 for a list to get you started.

You may wonder what your children will do during your Sabbath. Talk with your husband and see what works for your family. Trust me, while children resist naps, they often take wonderfully to a day of your rest. You off screens, relaxed, slowed down – this is their dream.

I let my children play and even go out front to enjoy time with the neighbors on Sabbath. My sons didn't sign up to be monks. I don't want them to resent Sabbath. I want them to come to cherish it. Some days we take a family mid-day nap if our Sabbath for that week is on Sunday. Sabbath supper often is either leftovers, barbeque, or a freezer meal in the crockpot. Taking a break from cooking is part of giving yourself a day off.

If, like me, you find yourself drifting from this practice of Sabbath, don't sweat it. You know just what to do. Look at the coming week; pick a day; receive and keep a sabbath rest.

Take Me Away

Finally, at least once a year, get away on a

personal retreat. Even better, if you are able, go two to four times a year. Pack your bags and get out of Dodge. This isn't a trip to an island to snorkel and watch hula dancers or a trek up a mountain in Nepal. Those experiences are quite fabulous and have their place in life. However, what we're talking about here is time to be still over an extended number of days (three or more is great if you can manage).

Your personal retreat doesn't have to break the bank. You can go through AirBnB or FaithStay. Monasteries often offer rooms at reasonable rates for people wanting solitude for a spiritual respite. You can even arrange with a friend or relative to stay at their home in a spare room. Just be sure they know you are there for retreat more than connection with others.

If going away really is beyond your financial capacity this year, you could set aside $10 a week from your grocery budget. In a year you will have $520 towards your next personal retreat. You may think you can't afford to get away. I'm here to say you can't afford not to.

The main point is to make space to be separated from all the daily demands, your electronics, and your people. It can be helpful to schedule a retreat with an organization where you will be guided through spiritual exercises and then given times alone to be still with God.

If the idea of three days alone spooks the daylights out of you, I hear you. Perhaps thoughts of which of your children will be cutting the other's hair or how they will survive on blue box macaroni and otter pops in your absence give you pause. Here's the thing. If you get away and are deeply replenished, you will come back (maybe to some level of re-entry chaos) with all those reserves to draw on as you bless your family.

If this feels like too big of a goal for now, set it aside. Come back to the idea after you've gotten comfortable with weekly Sabbath.

Leaving Margin

Beyond the daily break and the weekly practice of a day of rest, I want to share with you a way of looking at your time to help rest happen more easily. The concept of margin is easy enough to grasp. Look at the page you are holding in your hand. Around all the edges is a rim of white space. No words go there so our eyes can rest. Imagine the words crammed together and busting right up to the edge of the page. You may not notice margin when you read, but you sure would if it were missing.

Our overfilled lives cry out for margin like a poorly printed page. We must leave room around activities and tasks. As we go into chapters Twenty-Two through Twenty-Seven, I'm going to get more practical. Remember what I'm telling you here about margin. Space around the edges gives you wiggle room so you aren't rushed and packed in so tight. Leaving margin facilitates the growth of your restful spirit as you go about fulfilling your regular obligations.

If you want to practice including margin in your week, I suggest this exercise: Make your plan for the day, and then go back and cut two things out. Commit to doing this for one week. Do not put something else in the place of the items you remove. Leave the whitespace they create untouched.

When you find yourself with free time, ask yourself how it feels. You could even journal or note on your phone the way you experience having a less stressed schedule. Do you feel relief? Guilt? Anxiety? Restlessness? Freedom?

Change stretches us. Please don't give up when you feel uncomfortable. Keep your eye on the prize, and try this for a while until you adapt to a less pressured lifestyle.

<u>Make This Chapter Mine</u>

After reading this chapter, what stands out that I want to remember?

How can I build in times of rest daily, Sabbath weekly, and extended time away?

What are my barriers to consistently resting, and how can I eliminate those?

And Jesus said to them,
"Come away by yourselves
to a secluded place and rest a while."
~ Mark 6:31

"Come to Me, all who are heavy laden and are weary. I will give you rest."
~ Jesus

Chapter Eighteen

The Gifts of Rest

Rest is a gift. Rest also brings us blessings. One of the most immediate of these is perspective. When I was a little girl, I watched *Sesame Street*, a show on PBS. They used to sing a song on there that went, "That's about the size, where you put your eyes, that's about the size of it."

During the song the images would fade from a close up of a bug to way out over the earth and back again. This whole song was about perspective. We see things differently depending on how close or far away we are from them.

Taking a rest is like getting on an airplane and soaring over your circumstances. In Colossians God tells us to lift our eyes over the things of the earth and put them on the place where Jesus is seated with God the Father.[1] Perspective. We need time each day, week, month, and season to step back and gain perspective.

When an airplane lifts up, passengers peer down on what used to be day to day trouble as houses shrink into a patchwork quilt of neighborhoods. In the same way, we need to lift our eyes over our circumstances. To do this we have to build in times of separation. Even a short respite in your own bedroom for 15 minutes in the middle of the afternoon can work wonders on your attitude for the rest of the day. Don't believe me? Try it.

Centered

As much as I feel super exposed sharing this, I can become self-centered. I know I'm not alone. I don't spend hours looking in the mirror or think I'm the hottest thing since sizzling rice soup. I simply can end up with a mind that circles around me, my thoughts, concerns, and agenda. Another aspect of self-centeredness is self-importance. Just ugh. This is where we are sure things won't function without us. If we hold this belief long enough and actually act on it consistently, we subconsciously train the people around us to become more inefficient.

Awesome.

One of the huge blessings of rest is watching life flow without our input. We learn at a visceral level the truth: the world doesn't revolve around us. As valuable and cherished as each of us are, we are not pivotal, and, to be honest, that is a huge relief. I have experienced massive freedom when I stepped back and allowed things to go forward without me.

Intimacy with God

God didn't say, "Get busy and know I am God." Instead He says, "Be still,"[2] or even a more accurate interpretation of the Hebrew, "cease striving." Stop trying so hard and know He is God – your provider, your healer, your friend.

The phrase "cease striving" in the Hebrew gives an image of straw going into a fire or someone letting their hand fall down to their side. The phrase also refers to the end of a day when a person comes to relax. When we live in a pattern of busyness, our hearts are rarely still enough to truly connect with God. Let's learn to put our hands down, to allow time in our lives to know we aren't in charge, and to acknowledge God as the one who guards and guides us.

183

Trusting God is the heart of Sabbath. When we rest, we leave room to develop our relationship with Him in ways we simply can't when we are hustling around with activity.

Inner Refuge

Sometimes doing nothing is actually doing something very important. Solitude and silence cultivate a space of quiet within us. I see it as a sort of field where Jesus and I come together to rest. Every time I get away for a personal retreat, that field gains a few more acres. My capacity to sit with Him and hear His voice expands.

As I re-enter life, there's always the "Well now, that's over!" experience (partly because the people who all love and need me have not been on their own retreat). My tasks and deadlines also greet me. Nothing at home changes much while I'm away, but I come back with a few acres more of refuge contained within my heart.

Spirituality isn't meant to be kept on the mountaintop. We go there so we can return to the foothills, share what we have gained, and actually assimilate it in the trenches of life.

Finding Joy

Slowing down actually makes time seem to last

longer. Remember when you were a child and someone gave you a popsicle? I always took my time, enjoying all the sweetness lick by lick. I had friends who took a few chomps, caught the dropping remnants off their stick, and finished in no time. Not me. I made that popsicle last.

When we slow down, we make time last. Sometimes, in the middle of a day, just randomly I will pause and breathe deeply. This is my cue to myself to slow and savor. I take in what is around me. I cherish the people who are with me. That moment when I pause to breathe feels suspended in time. Joy is magnified when we slow.

The Paradox

As you think over the blessings of rest – perspective, a right view of your own importance, intimacy with God, cultivating an inner refuge, and a deep sense of joy – you might see what I see. All this striving and busyness often happens because we are pursuing these very blessings.

We think somehow if we work hard enough, say "yes" to all the things, and keep ourselves in the flow, we will find joy, peace, contentment, and deep love. Paradoxically, the secret lies in pulling back from so much activity and allowing ourselves to slow. It is there where deep longings will be fulfilled.

Adjusting Your Speed

Much like passengers in a car when the brakes are hit, we will feel the forward motion continue within us even after we intentionally slow. Some have called this the stirring of the silt in the river. When the water finally settles, the silt falls. For a while, your insides will not get the memo that you have slowed.

Don't quit. Stay slow and your heart will learn a new rhythm – one that is life-giving. Ironically, we become more focused and capable of doing things well when our pace is measured and we allow margin. We get more done when we work from a place of rest.

Make This Chapter Mine

After reading this chapter, what stands out that I want to remember?

What gifts of rest do I long for most?

How can I intentionally cultivate rest? Do I need to ask for support in getting more rest?

What fears do I have about resting? How realistic are those fears?

"Take My yoke upon you and learn from Me,
for I am gentle and humble in heart,
and you will find rest for your souls.
For My yoke is easy and My burden is light."
~ Matthew 11:29-30

*"Contentment doesn't mean I desire nothing,
but rather it's the simple decision
to be happy with what I have."*
~ Paula Rollo

Chapter Nineteen

More Isn't Always More

I don't know when it happened, but it did.
Contentment snuck up on me. For years I lived
oppressed by the lie that my happiness and
security existed just beyond the next
achievement or applause.

Fully Known, Fully Loved

The deepest longing of the human heart is to be
known and loved. I craved affirmation and
validation, yet didn't want you to know how
desperately I needed you to like me. I played it
cool. I lived with a private ache echoing off the
walls of my soul.

Over the years I have grown from performance-
based achievement to possessing a deep sense

of wellbeing in all the places that matter. So many factors have played into this transformation. My precious growing relationship with God trumps them all.

I tell women I mentor how I approached God like a stray dog. Having dodged cars on a freeway, been attacked by other animals, and nearly starved to death relying on my own ability to feed myself, I came to God suspicious and skittish.

As I sat with my mentor over the past 20 years, we worked through much of the doubt and mistrust, as well as distorted perceptions of God blocking me from intimacy with Him. Several good therapists and many gifted friendships have shored up shaky places in my heart along the way.

I used to read the Bible or pray to gain Christian good-girl points, check off a to-do list, and basically earn my way into His good graces. I overcommitted in ministry as a means of filling my spiritual resume. All this work aimed to secure me an economy ticket to God's presence. I knew all the first-class seats were taken.

God used the safe relationship with my mentor

and several others to serve as bridges between Himself and me. These people accepted me as I was. Perhaps God could too. As the walls I built for my own self-protection came down brick by brick, I drew nearer to God. Over the years I have come to know and depend on Him with a trust I only dreamed of having in those early years of my walk with Him. One day I looked around and realized I was content being me, right where I am.

Eugene Petersen had the audacious courage to translate the Bible. His translation, called *The Message*, contains this passage from Colossians:

> *Your old life is dead. Your new life, which is your real life—even though invisible to spectators—is with Christ in God. He is your life. When Christ (your real life, remember) shows up again on this earth, you'll show up, too—the real you, the glorious you. Meanwhile, be content with obscurity, like Christ.*[1]

The last sentence challenged me: Content with obscurity. When people pass me by, I am just A-Ok with it. Yep. I never thought I could say that and mean it, yet, here I am fully content with all I have, lacking nothing. The approval of people pales in comparison to the continuous attention and love of God.

It all boils down to the reality of Psalm 139 – a reflection of how fully known and loved we each are. God carefully made each of us how He wants us to be. He knows our thoughts before we think them. He numbered our days. He knows every thing we do. All that knowing – and He loves us fully. No condemnation (Romans 8:1); A love that goes to the cross for each one of us and so much more (Matt 7:11).

Those amazing Scriptures were mere words to me. Before my heart healed, they barely reached the soft places they intended to land. Over time I allowed God into those tender and vulnerable parts of me.

Foot in Mouth

On a walk towards the dorms on Biola campus at the Southern California Christian Writer's Conference, I started chatting with two women I had never met. They asked what I was writing. This is a common question writers ask one another – and they really want to hear the answer. When I told them about my first book, *Parenting Your Teen Through Chaos and Crisis*, I shared that I had self-published.

One of them asked me if it had been "successful." I said it was fruitful according to my definition of success. I had learned a lot, sold more books than I expected, and had been able to bless some moms with tools during a difficult season of motherhood. I quipped that I hadn't made the *NY Times* Best Seller List. Then I added, "I don't know if I would even want to make that list. Sometimes we writers fall into the trap of wanting more and more. We think our happiness hinges on selling a certain number of books or getting good reviews. We seek agents and publishers to get our book out to numerous people and then we are beholden to deadlines and have created a whole new hamster wheel for ourselves."

As we entered the lobby, I asked them if they were writers. It turns out one of them was an agent and the other a publisher. Smooth move, Patty. Yes, I did put my foot in my mouth just a little bit with those two sweet women. Note to self: find out if you are talking to an agent or publisher before critiquing the side effects of their profession.

Contentment in Smallness

The point I made remains valid and not just for writers. We all can fall into the trap of continually desiring more than we have. It's a recipe for discontentment. The hunger for more isn't always a terrible thing. Great achievements come from pressing on through difficulty and wanting to push the limits. Being famous isn't a curse or a blessing. It's just like everything else in life. You have to manage the downside while appreciating the perks.

That conversation solidified a thought I've been trying to crystalize. The things we often think "would be nice" never provide the answers to our heart's deepest longings. As Augustine said, "You have made us for Yourself, Oh Lord, and our souls are restless until they find their rest in You."[2] Our restless souls will not be filled with more money, more fame, more attention, or more likes on Facebook or Instagram.

Looking back over the years I have walked with Jesus, I realize I have learned Mary's secret. I am doing the most needful thing. I have abandoned "doing" for the sake of earning. I know how to prioritize what is most important and let so much fluff go.

If God grows my reach, that will be His decision. In the meantime, my regular prayer is: "I am a branch." He is the vine. I do nothing significant without Him. If I do something, you will know it's from God. I experience unspeakable freedom knowing I don't have to push or clamor my way upward. I don't have to make myself into something I'm not. I can simply be and show up to what God has planned.

Join me in this if you would. Set down your striving for more and look around yourself. Stop to take in your family, your home, your opportunities. More deeply, allow yourself to acknowledge the amazing and overwhelming love God has for you. Then be content to be small in light of that enormous goodness.

<u>Make This Chapter Mine:</u>

After reading this chapter, what stands out that I want to remember?

Do I think of myself as fully known and fully loved? How does this truth settle my soul?

What stands in the way of me accepting God's unconditional love of me?

Do I still strive for some sort of external approval or think that my contentment hinges on something outside of what I have?

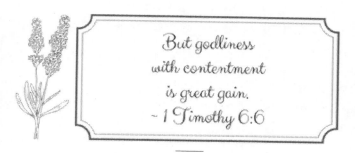

But godliness
with contentment
is great gain.
- 1 Timothy 6:6

"By being yourself you put something beautiful into the world that wasn't there before."
~ Edwin Elliot

Chapter Twenty

Finding Your Fit

When I was a child, my mom actually referred to my room as "the disaster zone." Every so often she would bravely instigate a cleaning day. This usually ended with me in tears as we combed through piles of papers and other messes for hours on end.

I experienced a life-quake crisis in seventh grade. The weekend after this event, I went through my room, cleaning and organizing everything, even adding labels. My reaction to the stress and pain in my inner world led me to attempt to gain control over my outer environment. I've been an organized person ever since.

Most of us don't undergo overnight transformations from hoarder to neat-freak. My experience has given me a unique perspective as to how different people react to clutter. When I started writing this book, I spoke with a number of friends. Depending on their personalities, they seemed to struggle with different aspects of time management and organization.

These conversations got me thinking more deeply about how many books about productivity and home organizing approach us as though we are all the same. As I said before, we won't find a one size fits all solution to living more intentionally and slowing our lives to a healthy pace.

As I was preparing this book, I developed a survey to understand the nuances better. I want to share what I learned with you. To keep this simple, I'm going to describe four general personality types. Then I'll share strengths and challenges each one faces when it comes to slowing, living intentionally, having a sense of purpose, and making the most of their time

See if you can identify with one or two of the personalities I describe. Throughout each description I will encourage you with some specific approaches tailored to your individual needs.

The Leader

If you are a leader, you might relate to the "Get-er-Done Girl" we talked about in Chapter Three. You have a bottom-line orientation. Knowing what needs to happen, you either delegate or implement what is required. You often work independently. Your confident, goal-oriented approach inspires trust and admiration in people around you.

Your strengths when it comes to intentional living are evident in the way you set and implement goals. You know your purpose and often filter decisions through it. Staying on task usually isn't a challenge for you. You focus and go for it.

A caution to you is to watch your boundaries. You are prone to take on more than you should because your sense of responsibility is high. When we get to the chapters on boundaries and planning, take special care to see where you can draw lines you haven't been as diligent about putting in place. Just because you can do something, doesn't mean it is yours to do.

Many of the women who define themselves as leaders told me they struggle with unrealistic and perfectionistic standards. They said these interfere with their ability to slow down. The biggest apprehension these women shared with me was the fear of failure. If you need to, go back to our chapter on perfectionism and re-read your notes (or the whole chapter!).

Women who lead told me they sometimes experience interruptions or distractions, and they do not like being taken off track. Anything (or anyone) who interferes with their original plan can be seen as an unwelcome interruption.

One woman said, "I manage time well. Too well! I drive my husband crazy because I'm very structured with every minute and never sit down." Another woman shared how systematized she was when her children were little. She said she wished she had taken more time to simply enjoy the moments. Can you hear the cry of her heart?

Do the people closest to you long for more of your presence? Will you look back on these years of motherhood wishing you had let more go so you could relish the goodness of time with those you love? Focus on what you can do to build rest and relationship into the life you are choosing for yourself.

Behind the Scenes Organizer

If you are very detail-oriented, you might be a behind the scenes organizer. If this is you, stability, accuracy, and logic give you a sense of comfort. You like people to stick to facts. When you face problems or decisions, you are prone to consider all the angles. Your cautious and meticulous nature causes you to attend to the particulars and follow the guidelines.

Like the leader, you easily set and monitor your own goals. You also know your purpose and tend to make decisions based on what you feel called to do. Even though you don't often consider yourself a leader, your natural sense of order causes you to manage your own time and the time of others around you. Sometimes you are alright with distractions. At other times, you resent the flow of your day being interrupted, especially if important tasks get set aside.

Unlike the natural-born leader, you may tend to procrastinate. Your attention to detail can make you spend too much time on decisions or implementing tasks. You also can be prone to take on more than you ought to out of a sense of duty to help others. You don't always ask for help when you need it. This can leave you finishing big jobs alone.

Women who are behind the scenes organizers face the biggest struggles making decisions. One woman shared with me, "I am currently in a state of analysis paralysis about my life." Another woman said she doesn't always discern what is important and what is not.

Like the leader personality, your tendency towards perfectionism can be a pitfall when it comes to organizing your time. You also experience a fear of failing. This can keep you from trying new things or from cutting back on your efforts when doing less could actually be good enough. As I mentioned to the leaders reading this chapter, you may want to go back and read the section on perfectionism and then start allowing yourself to experience the freedom of appropriate mediocrity.

Interestingly, your personality takes on the needs of others more easily than anyone else. When women spoke to me about this, they said things like, "I need to make myself a priority in my life." As moms this can be so hard. When we get to the chapter on self-care, take copious notes. Then ask a friend to check in with you regularly to make sure your color-coded to-do list has some time allotted for your own filling along with a consistent dose of weekly fun.

One other theme I noticed with the behind the scenes organizer was the way others around them tend not to be as organized. This can be a great source of discord and frustration. One woman shared this: "I love organization, but it bugs me when no one else sticks to my organization. I have just had to do what works best for my family and let go of my OCD-ness for everyone else." What wisdom! I know it takes a lot to release our need for order when others in the home aren't wired that way.

In our home we do a "clean sweep" several times a day. I simply announce those words and set a timer for the number of minutes I think tidying will take. If someone leaves items out for a longer period of time after having opportunity to pick them up, I confiscate them and put them in my closet until the coming Saturday. They can earn their things back that day.

I allow the boys to make messes in their own rooms. Once a week we do a clean-up day to make things somewhat orderly. I want the main rooms to stay regularly organized, so I enforce the system that works for all of us. Rather than constantly nagging, this sporadic tidying meets my needs and theirs.

I no longer require external order to calm my anxious heart. I still like a spit-spot home better than not, so I put these few practices in place to help us as a family. I decided I don't want my boys growing up with their most vivid memories of me being the times I chided them for messes. By letting go of my fastidiousness, I am able to delight in the people around me more fully while cultivating a home characterized by peace instead of criticism.

Loyal Peacemakers

Some people are fast-paced worker bees. Others are methodical and organized. If neither of these types describe you, it is possible you are more like my husband. Let me tell you about him.

My sweet man is more go-with-the-flow. He doesn't keep a calendar. Instead he has his "notes." He's not the planner type. When I have something crucial to tell him, he might jot it on a scrap of ragged paper. Later, in my nervousness, I'll ask, "Hun, don't forget to pick our son up at 3:00pm." He'll nonchalantly tell me, "I know. I have my note."

One year I gave him this beautiful leather planner. After a week I noticed he wasn't carrying it around. He decided to give it to a secretary who would actually make use of it.

If you are like my husband, you prefer a slower pace. People may describe you as easy going, though, internally you may not always feel as relaxed as you look. You appreciate security and longevity. Conversely, you dislike uncertainty and change. You are extraordinarily patient and such a good listener.

Some peacemakers have good goal-setting skills, while others fumble around discerning what goals to set. Most peacemaking women I spoke to have a sense of purpose. The interesting thing about your personality is how you tend to get distracted, yet veering from your original course doesn't bother you as it does most other people. Your mental vacations give you some of the downtime you crave.

Your personality is the most flexible of all the types. Because of this you easily bend to the priorities of others. In the moment, and even for quite some time, this may not bother you. When I talk more intimately with women who are go-with-the-flow types, they share that as they age they realize they regret having set themselves aside and wish they had been more courageous to explore what really matters to them personally.

I want to encourage you to take the risk and dream. I don't simply mean to daydream. I actually am inviting you to think about what matters to you and to take some action to pursue those priorities. Share your dreams with at least one trusted friend who can spur you forward. Realize you may have to disappoint some people along the way. They will live.

God made you unique with a contribution to give this world. I encourage you to explore your purpose with Him. Just because you are comfortable taking the back seat or blending into the background doesn't mean you don't matter. Your dreams or goals are as valuable as those of the more vocal people you know.

Actually, most of the people I know who share your temperament have a great deal of wisdom and compassion to share with the world. Because you aren't always busy talking, you spend a lot of time observing and evaluating. Your input matters.

Many go-with-the flow types may say, "I don't like planning." All this organization and setting alarms on a phone might feel stuffy or stodgy to you. I'm not here to convert you to a specific way of organizing your life so you engage in what is meaningful. I want you to make this process yours. I will ask you to step back and ask yourself if the way you are living is helping you move toward your dreams in order to live a life with few regrets.

The Life of the Party

This type of woman is naturally outgoing and energetic. You are a people person. Being enthusiastic, you love dreaming and are very present in the moment. You tend to be less detail oriented than others. You are a delight to your many friends.

When I spoke to women who have this personality type, their ability to set goals and stick to them varied quite a bit. One thing they shared in common was the tendency to live day-to-day without thinking too far down the road. They either immerse themselves in the task at hand or procrastinate because something more fun presents itself.

The biggest barrier these women shared with me was the ability to stay on task. One woman said, "I get distracted easily by all the bright, shiny objects." I also heard the common theme of lack follow through on things that matter to them. One woman shared her solution: "The best way for me to stay on task is to set my timer for a predetermined amount of time and make myself stay in that defined area until the timer goes off."

Life-of-the-party women resist slowing down when it means having increased time alone. Being with others ranks high on the priority list (if there is a list) for these social butterflies. When you read the chapters on rest, I hope you are inspired to override your need for constant companionship to make room for some much needed solitude.

Another alternative might be to find a friend

who also wants to slow her life and approach this together. Sometimes you can simply snuggle one of your children on the couch and be quiet together. This blesses your child while allowing you to cultivate some slowing down for your own soul.

Regardless whether you are a leader, organizer, peacemaker, or the life of the party, you can live more intentionally. God put amazing strengths in you as He planned your unique personality. Knowing yourself can help you customize the way you manage time so that you can make the most of the life you have been given.

Make This Chapter Mine

After reading this chapter, what stands out that I want to remember?

What ways does my unique personality help me live intentionally?

How do some of my personality traits get in my way?

What can I do to build in some support or make changes where needed?

> Therefore, since we are surrounded by such a great cloud of witnesses, let us throw off everything that hinders and the sin that so easily entangles. And let us run with perseverance the race marked out for us.
> ~ Hebrews 12:1

*"Planning is bringing
the future into the present
so that you can do something about it now."
~ Alan Lakein*

Chapter Twenty-One

According to Plan

I'm going to be totally up front with you from the start of this chapter. My intention is to convert you to the goodness of planning. What I won't do is try to force you into a specific style of goal setting and scheduling. Your personality and preferences will determine the form this takes for you. The aim of this chapter is to help you see the benefit of setting your sails.

If you already have a habit of planning, I hope to help you refine your skills. If you don't plan and live more according to the way the wind is blowing, this chapter can equip you to put some new habits in place.

Either way, let's remember planning is a tool. We never worship the tool. It is only something we use for a greater purpose. In this case, our aim is to live a more slow and intentional life so we can make room for what matters most.

The 90-Day Plan

Over the course of my blogging and writing, I have been a part of several mastermind groups. We meet every few weeks by video conference to celebrate one another's successes. Each member takes her turn sharing challenges or places she needs input. Then we brainstorm, give feedback, and end in prayer for one another.

This past year I was in overdrive during a certain season. I had a scheduled meeting with my mastermind group. One of the women noticed I was trying to sort through too many projects simultaneously. She shared a tool she learned from an organizational consultant. I immediately implemented 90-day planning. It has been one of the most helpful habits I have ever put in place.

The practice starts with me taking a week to prayerfully consider the coming 90 days. I begin by asking God to continue to clarify my overarching life purpose. I'm always growing in my understanding of how He formed me and what He is calling me to do with my life.

With my life purpose in mind, I ponder the coming 90 days. I think through all the options of where I could invest my time and energy. I evaluate my goals. I sort through opportunities. I remember my priority in each major area of my life. Then I determine what my focus will be for the coming 90 days.

After I hone in on what matters most, I choose my yes and no answers. I carefully decide where I will spend my time for the coming 90 days. As Greg McKeown, author of *Essentialism*, says, we need to determine the vital few things we are really called to do as opposed to spending our time in the trivial many. Otherwise, as he observes, we will end up making a millimeter of progress in one million directions.[1] When we hone in on a smaller focus, we can apply ourselves well.

When new opportunities come my way, I hold those up to the focuses I already laid out to see whether a new event or task fits into my life for this season, or if it needs to wait. Sometimes I may decide to reconfigure my 90-day plan.

Usually, however, I table new opportunities until the coming planning week, which I schedule at the end of each given 90 days.

I'll give you an example of how this has worked in my current 90-day segment of life. The second week of April I clarified my goals. I knew I wanted to put a lot of time into the book and courses for *Slow Down, Mama!* I also wanted to focus on a few specific things with each of my sons and in my marriage. I prayed over relationships (from my "to-love" list) and determined what I would do to pursue those people intentionally.

Personally, I have been trying to get in better shape and eat in a healthier manner, so those goals were high on the list for the 90 days. I also knew what I was working on spiritually and what books I wanted to read to support my other goals. Since I'm focusing on *Slow Down, Mama!*, I am reading books about intentional living. Ok, I'm devouring them at a rate of one book a week!

The last book I wrote came out at the end of February. Some friends had told me they really wanted it in Audiobook. I was tempted to make a recording for their sake (and for anyone else who would make use of that format). I also had several invitations to speak and a few other writing opportunities.

As those choices came forward, it was easy to table them onto the list "Consider for Next 90 Days." All but one speaking engagement simply didn't fit with the other priority items I had determined for this season. To say yes would gobble time I needed to protect for my most important tasks and people. I just may complete an audiobook in the coming 90–day period. I'll evaluate that in my next designated planning week. Meanwhile I don't have to give it any thought.

The minimization of stress and lack of decision fatigue I experienced convinced me of the value of this practice of 90–day planning. Just as we use our personal purpose statement to sort our yes and no answers, we can use this 90–day plan to filter choices as we go through life.

I don't count the week between each 90 days as a part of the 90 days to come. It is a separate week of its own. I sometimes am able to plan a day or three away during that planning and clarifying week. That is ideal when it can work.

Planning Your Week

Knowing my priorities for each 90-day section of life helps me screen what can and cannot fit into most weeks. I spend about 30-40 minutes every weekend planning out the week to come. Setting aside a time to plan could feel like a luxury or a waste of time, but it truly pays back way more than it takes.

When I sit down, I look at obligations we already have carefully chosen to include in our life. I map out blocks of time to complete work, writing, and school planning. Then, I fit in components of my 90-day goals such as fitness, special projects, or prioritized relationships. I go back over the week after planning it to ask myself if there is enough margin and flexibility. If a week is too full, I start thinking through what can be postponed or cancelled.

The simple practice of planning the week ahead provides a road map. You may feel energized by this practice. On the other hand, you may feel cramped and stifled. If you don't like planning in time slots, how about making a list of things you would like to get done in the given week, and then designating days to complete those? As Greg McKeown says, "If you don't prioritize your life, someone else will."[2]

What's in Your Plan?

Let's talk about your plan. We discussed the importance of daily and weekly times of rest. I can't emphasize this enough. Without margin between events or intentional downtime, you set yourself up for burnout. As you plan your week, I suggest you put rest in as though it's an appointment. The most effective and productive people in the world rest often and guard their rest with diligence.

Next, I want to encourage you to include times for planning. Your week won't plan itself – or it will! That's even worse. When time rolls on without direction, you live at the whim of others around you. Every task or opportunity seems to bear the same weight and you can easily feel pulled in hundreds of directions.

What has blessed me most has been to engage in all the levels of planning, starting with continually refining my sense of life purpose. The 90–day plan and weekly plan provide structure to ensure my mission in life fits into the day-to-day.

To make sure my plan fits within reality, I set aside about five minutes every night to review the day to come. In the morning, as I sit with coffee on the back porch, I spend time in prayer and devotion. Following that, I review my plan for the day once more to see if anything needs to be changed.

When Plans and Life Collide

Even with all this planning, life never goes as planned. People have needs which rightly intersect our original thoughts for how the day would go. Children get sick; we get sick; events cancel or are rescheduled. We have to flex our plans or have a plan B when life doesn't flow the way we anticipated.

In Proverbs God reminds us: "Many are the plans in a man's heart, but the Lord's purpose will prevail."[3] That should be a comfort to us. We plan the best we know how with the limited view and information we have. God will direct our steps and what He knows is best will come to pass.

Ultimately, the most important things are up to

Him. That is why we are advised "Commit your works to the Lord and your plans will be established."[4] Seeking His guidance as we plan and thinking about the purposes and callings He has placed in our lives helps us plan in a way that lines up with His will.

His overarching involvement doesn't mean we shouldn't plan. It simply means we need to pray as we plan and then hold our plans loosely.

Having a plan is like having a map when you go on a trip. You may hit a road block and change course, but the map got you that far, and you needed it to give you direction towards your destination.

Plan well, travel well.

Make This Chapter Mine

After reading this chapter, what stands out that I want to remember?

How can I include 90-day planning and weekly planning in my life?

What can I do to include plans to rest regularly?

How can I work in a "plan B" when life interferes with what I had planned?

"All the paths of the Lord are steadfast love and faithfulness, for those who keep His covenant and his testimonies."
~ Psalm 25:10

"It's how you spend your time in the day to day that will get you to your destination."
~ Darin Rowse

Chapter Twenty-Two

Day by Day

How many of our days as moms can tend to drone on in seemingly insignificant activities? Life tends to gravitate towards the mundane or demanding. Meanwhile we lose sight of what makes life meaningful.

Your Days Matter

Your life, no matter how routine and small it feels, is huge to those closest to you. The way you provide a safe haven for your children, create a home for those you love, welcome friends, and give of your time matters greatly to those who depend upon you. It may seem you are only folding towels and wiping up messes, but your faithfulness to show up and be a constant in the lives around you is forming a foundation in their hearts.

I hope, as we identified your "to be," "to love," and "to do" (purpose), you feel more motivated to infuse each day with meaning. Doing something for the right reason can energize us. Laying hold of our "why" can change everything. One of the best ways to be sure we live out our deeper purposes is to plan them into each day.

After we have clarified our 90-day vision and have created a weekly schedule, it doesn't take much to map out a daily plan. What I do is to look over the coming day the night before. I think about what matters most in that day. I might even put stars near those events or tasks. I make sure the people and purposes most valuable have space in that day.

When I lay out the week, I designate certain days for specific priorities. That way, when I begin planning any given day, I already know what fits best according to the overall view of my season and my week.

Morning and Evening

Another aspect of planning has been including a morning and evening routine. I'm not rigid about this, but I do plan it in. I try to have a relatively consistent bedtime (around 10:00pm) and waking time (around 5:30am). I also have a rhythm of what I do when I wake and before I go to sleep. Sometimes I'm better about sticking to the routine than others.

The benefit of this practice is that I include a lot of habits that tend to go to the wayside when I live more by the seat of my pants. I wash my face, put on moisturizer, read, etc. In the morning I have a time of quiet for prayer and reading spiritual materials. I do a plank before getting dressed. Many of those things go out the window when I'm more loosey-goosey about my day.

I recently worked one more thing into my morning routine. I snuggle up in bed and don't start the morning's activities right away. There's something about not jetting out of bed that sets a tone for the day. I realize I have enough time to linger. I am not in a rush.

Having a routine or schedule doesn't mean we must live hurried and obligated to it. Our plan is another tool. It serves to make sure what we want most fits into the rhythm of our days. Never blindly follow your calendar as though it were the boss of you. You own your time. It is a gift to you to spend well.

Your Unique Routine

Having a rhythm blesses us because we are, by nature, creatures of habit. We learn to automatically implement activities that we have meant to be in our day. This creates less mental stress and strain. We know we will get to each vital element. Habits can be strung together one after another. Our children also learn to do things in a pattern, such as putting on pjs and then brushing their teeth. Having predictable rhythms makes children less anxious, which diminishes their acting out.

I want to make a suggestion regarding your personality and how you structure your morning and evening routines. If you are the detail-oriented type of personality, you will like a structured plan to the start and end of your days. Go for it!

If you are more introverted or have a deeper need for solitude, be sure to carve out some quiet time alone as you start your day and before you go to bed. The concept of extended privacy may seem unrealistic as a mom. It can be challenging but is not impossible. You may have to solicit support, get up earlier, or give your children something engaging to do in order to grab some private moments, but it will pay off if it means you getting what you need before you head into a day filled with people who need you.

If you are the life-of-the-party girl, you probably don't like things to be the same every day. While monotony comforts the more structured personality types, nothing makes you cringe more than predictable sameness. I encourage you to build in variety so you don't end up feeling confined or bored. Planning themed time blocks works well. Then change what goes into those each day.

For example, you might have a rhythm of connecting with God, exercising, getting dressed, and then moving into the rest of your day. Some days your time with God might include a prayer walk. On other mornings you could sit with a devotion or practice Lectio Divina. Your exercise time might change from a Zumba class to swimming. Keep yourself interested by switching up details while keeping the rhythm consistent. You also may want to consider including people in your routine to fulfill your love of all things social.

Staying in the Day at Hand

One of the biggest gifts I have received in the past few years has been the increasing capacity to be present in the day at hand. Our brains so easily drift into the past, cultivating resentment and regret, or the future where we borrow trouble and fear. Even if we spend time dreaming about what is to come, we often miss the precious goodness right in front of us. I have found three mindsets to help us stay present.

Be Still

During a particularly trying day, God whispered, "Exodus 14:14" into my heart. I wasn't clear what that verse said (though I may have known in the past). I turned to it and was astounded to hear Him saying, "The LORD will fight for you; you need only to be still."[1]

You might wonder how this verse relates to time management and learning to live in the day at hand. When I face difficulties, I am tempted to mentally run ahead. When I do, I live in the future while leaving God in the dust. In my fears

I concoct worst case scenarios. Those imaginings rarely include God and His ever-present hand of care, protection, and guidance. When I remember that I only need to stand while He fights for me, I remain centered in the day at hand.

Manna for Motherhood

At one point during the 40-year trek through the desert, God gave the Israelites manna – their daily provision. They couldn't store it up, yet they never needed fret about the coming day. The manna they needed was ready each morning to meet their need.

I have come to realize God gives manna of all sorts. The word "manna" means "what is it?". The Israelites had no idea what manna was. We can feel the same sort of befuddlement at His means of providing for our needs. Sometimes we may receive a provision from God and think, "What is this you have given me God?"

If we trust Him, we will find His provision to be just what we need, right when we need it. We never lack what we need most. God lovingly scatters daily manna for our motherhood. All we need to do is faithfully receive it.

This Day Alone

Recently, God has shown me something about how He guides me. In Matthew it is recorded how Jesus taught the crowd about staying in the day at hand. He said, "Each day has enough trouble of its own."[2] In Psalm 139, one of my favorite and most comforting spots to go in Scripture, God tells us He has our paths marked out, and He guides us every step of the way.[3]

In Psalm 119 He says His Word is a lamp unto our feet and a light unto our path.[4] In the days when that was written, men would tie little candles to their sandals when they walked in the dark. The light from the candle only illuminated the step or two ahead. They had just the light they needed to take the next stride forward.

We too receive our guidance as a light unto our path. Sometimes we get a glimpse of the greater length of the journey ahead, but most often, our current path is lit so we can focus immediately ahead of where we stand and safely walk into what is next based on the light given.

Make This Chapter Mine

After reading this chapter, what stands out that I want to remember?

How can I implement or strengthen my morning and evening routines?

What do I want to remember about God's daily provision and guidance?

"All the paths of the Lord are steadfast love and faithfulness, for those who keep His covenant and his testimonies."
~ Psalm 25:10

*"Focus is a matter of deciding
what things you are not going to do."*
~ John Carmack

Chapter Twenty-Three
I Ate That

I have learned some invaluable tools for navigating times when life starts to shoot bags of ping-pong balls at me rapid fire. You know the feeling. Sometimes we are so bombarded with requests, demands, and obligations our brain literally goes into fight-flight, and we lose the capacity to discern and choose well. At times like this, I employ the "Brain Dump." Since learning this technique I have taught other moms and executives of companies to use it.

The Beauty of the Brain Dump

To complete a Brain Dump, get out a piece of paper or turn on the microphone on your cell and let it all out. Start listing every task or obligation in a stream of consciousness. Don't filter or sort, simply pour out everything that is on your mind. What do you have to do? Where do you have to be? List the minutia and the monstrosities.

Over the years I've created a form divided into eight quadrants for my personal Brain Dump. I keep copies in a section in my planner for quick access any time I need one. In each square section of the paper I have a title related to an area of my life: Family, Homeschool, Work, Writing, Ministry, Household, Friendship, Personal. As I dump out "to-dos" and scheduled activities onto the paper, I put them under the category where they fit.

After emptying my brain onto paper, I can sit back with my right mind reengaged. I then evaluate all these tasks and obligations. I'll show you how. The point is to decide which commitments are unavoidable or line up with your vital priority and then to put those on the calendar to ensure they get done.

I call this my "I Ate That" approach to sorting out my Brain Dump. You'll see why. The method involves four steps to sorting through the Brain Dump list once it has been generated. If you dictate your Brain Dump into your phone or plop all your thoughts on paper you can sort and simplify your list with this approach. At the end of the process your sense of overwhelm will diminish and your clarity will be restored. The four steps are Evaluate, Eliminate, Delegate or Collaborate, and Procrastinate.

Evaluate

During the Evaluate step, you look over your list. By breaking mine into categories, I can look at each one separately. I call to mind my 90-day plan and my overarching purpose. I use a method I learned in the 1980s when I had a Franklin planner.

I sort by A, B, C importance. I write "A" next to any task or needing to be done today, anything unavoidable, and anything critically needed. An "A" also goes by anything lined up with my greater purpose and 90-day priority.

I then give "B" ratings to things that are important, but not needed to be done immediately or not completely lined up with my goals and priority. Then I give a "C" to everything that would be nice, but is not essential. Maybe those things will be more important down the road, but in this day, they can wait and are not in line with what is vital to me and those I love.

Eliminate

The next step is to eliminate. Once I have sorted my list into A,B,C levels of importance, I can decide what to cross off my list. Life constantly presents alternatives. We can easily end up swamped with choices and opportunities. To complicate matters, we have ready access to opinions and input from many people and sources. During this step of the "I Ate That" process, I eliminate everything that is not going to fit in my week. I either put those on a "maybe later" list, or I just kick them to the curb.

Let's bear in mind a key concept: we won't do all the things. We can't have it all. We must choose well. Eliminating what shouldn't be on our list isn't losing something, it is actually making room to gain a great deal. Instead of trying to be it all and do it all, we can now focus well on what is really ours to do. We know what matters most, and we put that front and center.

The other part of the eliminate step is to purge fluff. Here's an example. My son's friend has a birthday coming up. We could buy a big gift, shopping around to find what is perfect, craft a homemade card, and then wrap it all better than the sales woman at Nordstrom, take a snapshot, and post it on both Pinterest and Instagram. That's great on a week when we have the time to invest.

The "fluff" makes this gift personalized and from the heart. Sometimes the fluff makes mom into a mom-ster. Grumbling and stressed we run through the store; returning home we insist on a Michelangelo creation on the front of the card. Everyone is miserable, and we're frazzled.

Instead, we can grab a gift card or a box of Legos, buy the card, and put it in a gift bag. Eliminating fluff also reduced all the crazy. So, while I look at the things to cross off my list, I also ask myself what can get by with my B-minus effort and still be perfectly acceptable given what needs my A+ effort and attention.

Delegate or Collaborate

The next step in the "I Ate That" process involves two choices. I either delegate what can be done by others around me or collaborate what can we do together. Many tasks do not have to be done by me. When it comes to housework, I do chores with my children until they are proficient and then I assign them jobs. My husband pitches in running errands or completing a homecare project. I share ministry and workloads.

Collaborating has come to be one of my favorite things in the world. We are often exponentially more creative and effective when we join forces. I collaborate in our homeschooling with other moms. We team teach co-ops and host events together. I collaborate in blogging and writing – marketing for others, guest writing, and soliciting support in projects. My husband and I collaborate our parenting efforts and each bring our unique perspective and approach to the process.

As you sort your tasks, ask yourself, "Who else could do this?" or "With whom could I join forces to get this done better?" A burden carried by more than one person is automatically lighter.

Procrastinate – Yep, Really.

Finally, I procrastinate. This term has such a negative connotation. Literally, it means to put off what can be put off until tomorrow. In Latin the term *pro* means *forward*, and *cras* means *tomorrow*. How many times do we get bogged down bringing tomorrow's business into today? As a matter of fact, Jesus tells us not to borrow trouble from tomorrow.[1] We need to put tomorrow's tasks where they belong.

Yes, certain projects require we chip away at bits and pieces consistently over time so we don't approach a deadline with an insurmountable amount of work left. In many cases, though, we can put something off for another day. That frees us up to do only what needs to be done in the day at hand. Healthy procrastination is a great tool when it comes to minimizing stress.

Finally, when you have evaluated, eliminated, delegated, collaborated, and appropriately procrastinated your brain dump, you can put the remaining tasks into your calendar or back onto your streamlined to-do list, and start to actually get them completed with much more of a sense of energy and focus.

Living on Autopilot

If you know about how autopilot works on a plane, you can understand it isn't a matter of simply setting a course and going to sleep. In the process of depending on autopilot, the plane continually veers to the right and is reset to course, then veers to the left, and is redirected. Throughout the flight, a constant recalibration occurs, keeping all things heading in the originally determined direction. In order for us to stay the course with our plans, we also need to master the art of recalibrating.

Scheduling our priority and determining which tasks line up with our purpose and capacity isn't a "one and done" experience. Life is fluid, so we have to adjust accordingly. We start with a plan. Then we veer from the routine. As life changes, our time demands are altered and we have to flex to revamp what was working.

Don't feel badly when the wheels start to seem to fall off. Step back and re-apply the basic principles you know work. Think about your purpose and revisit your 90-day plan. Brain dump, sort with the "I Ate That" approach, and get a workable plan for your days and weeks. We will get derailed at times. We can get back on track.

After reading this chapter, what stands out that I want to remember?

How can I make use of a brain dump when I feel overwhelmed?

How will I remember the four steps to "I Ate That? (Evaluate, Eliminate, Delegate/ Collaborate and Procrastinate)

What tends to overwhelm me most?

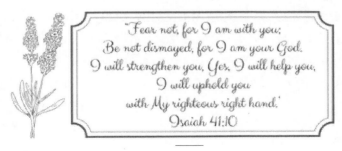

"Fear not, for I am with you;
Be not dismayed, for I am your God.
I will strengthen you, Yes, I will help you,
I will uphold you
with My righteous right hand."
Isaiah 41:10

*"It's not about making the right choice.
It's about making a choice
and making it right."*
~ J.R. Rim

Chapter Twenty-Four

To Do, or Not to Do? ...

I was walking on the treadmill at our gym this past winter. A friend had just told me to check out Emily P. Freeman's podcast. We were going through a family crisis at the time, and my energy level had taken a nosedive. I hadn't remembered to adjust my expectations of myself to match the decrease in my capacity.

As I listened to Emily's soothing voice, she said she was here for those of us who struggle with decision fatigue. I felt known. Had she witnessed the barrage of challenges in my life over the past few months? Emily shared her hesitation about a choice to go to the Philippines with Compassion International.[1] Revealing her fear of flying, she let us in on the key question she now asks herself before making every important decision: "Am I being led by love or pushed by fear?"

Love or Fear?

Have you ever heard a sentence and found it weaving its way your lifestyle? Listening to Emily's question was one of those moments. I had been intentionally rooting out fear over the past 20 years as a part of my healing journey with God. Despite my diligence, when she contrasted fear and love in light of decision-making I had a huge "aha" moment.

Before I go into the ways we best make choices, I want us to really solidify this undergirding principle. For every decision, let's pause and ask ourselves if we are being fueled by love or fear. It makes all the difference in the world when we know our heart motivation.

Know your Purpose

As we continually clarify our purpose and what is vital for us, making decisions becomes less daunting. I keep emphasizing knowing your purpose throughout the book so it becomes second nature to you. I believe it serves as the best filter for decision making.

Most of us don't determine our purpose clearly and with finality as a one-time event. We are constantly refining and discerning our purpose over the course of our lifetime.

My experience has been a "go with what you know" approach. I move forward based on what I think seems to be my deepest purpose, and as I do, I find out more about myself and how I am meant to be spending this gift of a life.

When you determine the people you want to invest in (your to-love list), character traits you want to cultivate (your to-be list), as well as the specific places you are called and gifted (your to-do list), you can hold any choice or activity up to those criterion to determine more clearly if it should be a "yes" or "no."

As I have been offered increasing opportunities to speak to groups of women, I use the filter of my purpose to help me choose when to accept and decline. If I have been on the road a lot, I know my priority of devoting time to my family is getting less attention. At times like this I temporarily turn down opportunities to talk so I can invest in my husband and boys.

As I mentioned before, I continue to cultivate

gentleness and a spirit of encouragement in my character. To be as sweet as I can, I need to allow margin and rest. As I look at offers to write or speak, I have to ask myself if I will be left with enough downtime to be my best self. If not, I immediately say "no thank you" to the request. Nothing is more important to me in this season of life than being a gentle and loving presence in my family. The filter of purpose makes decision making easier.

Plan to Decide

Some of you have a five-year plan, ten-year vision, and written goals for this year with measurable outcomes. You scheduling rock stars don't need me to tell you the value of looking ahead and setting out a road map of where you are going. If anything, you may need encouragement to dial your planning back a tad to let things flow sometimes.

If you are inclined to live more in the day-to-day, I want to inspire you here. You may not love the process of planning, but you will be blessed by the results. Effective planning diminishes decision fatigue. You don't have to use Google Calendar and the Reminder App to make plans. You can plan your life your way.

I do want to ask you a few key questions if you are averse to planning. Is your life going the direction you want? Do you make time for what matters most? Are you able to say "yes" to your priority without getting dragged into trivial pursuits? If those three questions receive a resounding "yes," then you may have a method to your madness. As the queen of England says, "Carry on."

Most of us need to think ahead and make room for the most vital activities and precious relationships. If we don't, we risk the tyranny of the urgent and the domination of minutia. As I walked you through the three levels of planning in my life, I shared the way having 90-day, weekly, and daily plans allows me to eliminate a lot of confusion and potential options.

Decisions Cost Something

Over time I have deeply internalized the truth that I won't do it all. As a result, I am automatically more serious about making each choice count. I have to be willing to give many "no" answers, to miss out, and to let really awesome things pass me by.

I'm the girl who stood at the edge of the ocean, bearing the weight of an overextended life, too fearful of missing out to choose well. God has transformed me into a woman who lives intentionally. My life is characterized by the freedom He intends for all of us.

I chose to work as a part-time entrepreneur so I could be present for our boys while they were young. People in our extended family encouraged me and my husband to put my degree and talents into full-time, paying work. They set financial goals in front of us and told us we could only meet those if I would work full-time and enrol our boys in public school.

Had I done that, we could have travelled more as a family, put additional money aside for retirement, and eaten out at better restaurants. We chose to miss that boat with all the perks it offered. Looking back, I don't regret for a minute the job opportunities I turned down to stay home with our boys. I made sacrifices. What we gained far outweighs anything we lost.

Making Small Decisions

Small decisions should take very little time. Having a plan helps this. For example, when I started the habit of planning meals for the week ahead, I didn't face the drain of trying to figure out what was for supper night by night. As a part of my weekly planning, I look at the rhythm of each day to determine whether I should cook with the crock pot, ask my husband to barbeque, order out pizza or tacos, or cook a homemade meal.

Having the plan laid out for the week has reduced my stress. At times I even used a weekly format: Mondays were crockpot nights, Tuesdays were Mexican, Wednesdays were fish and veggies, etc. Then I simply filled in details under that theme for the given night each week. This helped me plan each week's meals more quickly.

When it comes to relatively insignificant decisions, it can sometimes boil down to picking the easiest choice by asking yourself what would make you feel less overwhelmed. Go with that answer when the decision isn't very critical. Saving energy by choosing the simple option leaves you freed up for deeper thinking on more important decisions.

In meal planning, I've had to forgo elaborate

meals in many seasons. If your call and gifting is cooking gourmet meals, you may need to simplify other areas of life to make room for longer hours spent in your kitchen. The point is to determine where you want to invest your life, and then keep other areas simple so you have freedom to go all in where it matters most.

Just Say "No"

Think about this: Small decisions should mostly be no answers. Does this sound crazy? Consider the overwhelm we feel when all options seem equally possible and good. This "just say no" rule of thumb can help you greatly. If you always plan to say no to any disruptions to your day, then you have to really be persuaded something is more important than your plans before you let it derail you.

I'm not saying things can't supersede our predetermined plans. Intrusions do occur regularly. We shift gears when it is warranted. Having an attitude that only worthy things can bump the planned schedule helps us screen more carefully.

The Two-Minute Rule

Another great tip for making small decisions is

to use the two-minute rule when possible. If something small comes across your day – such as the thought that you need to stamp and address a response letter for a wedding – just do it.

If the task will take fewer than two minutes to finish, doing it gives you the sense of completion without wasting time and energy putting it off. You don't need to spend more time later trying to remember it and fitting it into your schedule.

I used to write long lists of every trivial to-do item that crossed my path. Just looking at the list overwhelmed me. Since instigating the two-minute rule, my to-do list only contains more meaty items. It is far shorter and truly achievable.

Make This Chapter Mine:

After reading this chapter, what stands out that I want to remember?

Do I tend to make decisions from a place of love or fear?

How does knowing my purpose help me decide well?

How does knowing I won't do it all impact the way I view what I choose? Can I think, "no" first?

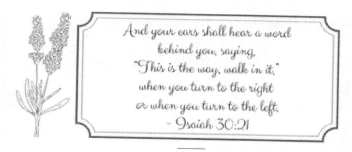

And your ears shall hear a word
behind you, saying,
"This is the way, walk in it,"
when you turn to the right
or when you turn to the left.
~ Isaiah 30:21

"Remember the decisions you make determine the schedule you keep. The schedule you keep determines the life you live. And how you live your life determines how you spend your soul."
~ Lysa TerKeurst

Chapter Twenty-Five
Making Big Decisions

Depending on the complexity of the issue, big decisions require more time because they entail thinking about long and short-term goals and your deepest purposes.

Our biggest decisions require us to ask ourselves questions like the ones Greg McKeown shares in *Essentialism*.[1] Focusing on what we love and are truly called to do provides us laser focus during decision making. Using the analogy of a closet, he reminds us most of our attempts to purge clothing rotate around questions like "Will I use this down the road?"[2]

Instead, we need to ask harder questi̶o̶n̶s̶. am I hanging onto this? Do I love it? W̶ I do or pay to obtain it if it weren't min̶ process of deciding about events and obligations needs to be even more rigorous than decisions about what fills our closet.

A Change of Scenery?

A few years ago, one of my dearest friends moved two hours away towards the coast. My husband grew up at the beach, and I tease him he is like a Saint Bernard dog in the snow when it comes to being around the ocean. He simply comes to life near the salty air and watery horizon.

We started considering relocating shortly after my friend moved. So many factors went into this decision. First of all, we factored in the ages of our boys and their roots in the only hometown they had ever known. Secondly, we had to think through the capacity we had to make a viable income and pay a higher cost of living. Thirdly, we considered our connection to our home church and friendships in this community.

While we had wanted to be closer to the beach for many years, we ultimately realized this ecision didn't line up with the deeper things God was calling us to in this season of our life as a family.

We visit the ocean once every month or two. Those getaways refresh us partly because we aren't living at the beach every day of our lives. Yes, God would provide other areas for us to minister if we moved, but we truly feel called to serve in the places He has placed us here. The financial capacity to move was possible, but not guaranteed. By filtering our choices through our purposes and capacities, we were clear it was a "no" for now.

The Early Bird Gets the Worm

I've heard it said we should make our big decisions in the morning – when our brains are more alert. Science backs this up. My own experience does as well. I have noticed I can get work that requires ingenuity done almost twice or three times as quickly if I tackle it in the morning.

This morning freshness tends to be equally true of night-owls and early birds. The difference is a person who stays up late tends to experience their "optimal" morning brain power somewhere around 9:30 or 10:00am due to the sluggish feeling when they first awaken. You may want to play around with this to find your optimal time.

Your Go-To Method

Another key I have heard and implemented is to have a decision making rubric or pattern and stick with it. Trying on various approaches to decision-making causes each decision to be a fresh learning process. This wastes time and energy.

If we acquire a series of questions or steps to use every time we face a major decision and practice these with consistency, we will find the process becomes second nature, and our stress is diminished. We also become far more skilled at discerning between options the more we run choices through our system for decision making. Pick a method that works for you and make it your go-to.

Alli Worthington shares her "Five F's" of decision making in her funny, practical, and self-revealing book, *Breaking Busy*. She suggests we filter our choices through Faith, Family, Future, Fulfillment, and Friends. She asks these questions:

- Does this align with your faith?
- How does this affect your family?
- Think of the future you in 10 weeks, 10 months, 10 years. Will you be happy with this decision or regret it?
- What are you most fulfilled doing? Will this decision bring you feelings of happiness or resentment down the road?
- What do my most trusted friends say about this decision? [3]

Chase It Down

One thing Lysa TerKeurst recommends in her book *The Best Yes* is to "chase the decision down."[4] This simple practice involves considering the outcomes of the choice before you. When you realize where the decision will lead, what you will potentially gain, and what you will inevitably have to give up, you can decide more clearly if the decision is a "yes" or "no" for you.

One example of this happened over this summer. Many of our homeschool years have included co-ops for learning science or going on field trips. Each summer I re-evaluate what we will commit our time doing for the coming school year. As I thought about the potential for learning science with a group, I chased the decision down.

Spending two Wednesdays a month in group classes with fewer families participating this year would mean more of my time spent planning and teaching than in previous years. I would have to set aside other learning to make room for science preparation.

I talked with another mom, and we decided to modify what we are going to do. We will only meet once a month to conduct science experiments related to all the reading and learning we will do separately in our homes. This will provide group learning which can be so fun and really enhance the experience for the children, meanwhile it also will free us up from all the planning and prep a more frequent class would require.

Chasing the decision down gave me the insight as to what I would gain and lose, so the decision became clear in a matter of a day rather than taking weeks to determine.

DWYWD

In my book *Parenting Your Teen Through Chaos*

and Crisis I shared the acronym DWYWD which stands for Decide What You Will Do.[5] Parenting expert, Jane Nelson, teaches this amazing key to discipline.[6] I have found it to be invaluable in decision making as well. Basically the premise centers around us not being able to control other people. We can, however, decide what we will do in light of what they do.

Sometimes our decision fatigue comes from wanting others to change. In parenting this can be especially true. We want our husband to be more compassionate with our children, or more stern and consistent. We hope our children will stop a certain behavior or character defect.

I unwittingly have wasted a great deal of time focusing on changing others in the past. These efforts were rarely consciously plotted. I found myself saying or doing things to try to influence the people closest to me to change the way they were acting without even realizing my motives. We all do this at least a little.

Healthy parenting includes teaching our children over time better ways to behave. Regardless of your overall philosophy of parenting, DWYWD can be an amazingly helpful tool.

When I learned DWYWD, it was literally life-changing. Sometimes instead of disciplining, we react from our emotions when our child misbehaves, or we make empty threats such as, "Stop that or you will be grounded for the rest of the day." These two common parenting defaults don't effect change as much as they cause frustration for everyone involved.

Jane Nelson's DWYWD approach says instead of engaging in power struggles, plan what you will do and notify in advance by saying things like:

- "When the table is set, I will serve dinner."
- "I will help with homework on Tuesday and Thursday, but not last minute."
- "When chores are done, I will drive you to your friend's house."

Then you follow through on your plans with kindness and firmness.

With DWYWD we aren't making sure our children bring homework to us, do chores, or set the table through our manipulation of the outcome. Instead, we tell our children what will happen, and we simply do what we said we would do. If they do their chores, they may go to their friend's. No chores? We don't leave until they are complete.

It usually only takes one or two times of our child testing whether we mean what we say for them to learn we are serious. Meanwhile we haven't yelled, laid out empty threats, or punished them in anger. I hope you are getting a glimmer of the freedom you obtain when you use this approach.

The house stays much calmer when we apply DWYWD. One key is to completely release your investment in the choice the other person makes. It takes patience, but you will find yourself with so much more peace in your heart as you practice this approach.

DWYWD in Your Marriage

Deciding what you will do applies in all areas of our life. A friend of mine is one of the people I first go to when my husband and I are having a rough patch in our marriage. She does the same with me. We confide in one another because we know we turn one another back towards our marriages, and we never bash one another's husbands, but we do sympathize and pray when things are difficult.

One year her husband was being very distant towards her and overly focused on work projects. She longed for more connection, but knew she couldn't make him do anything differently. When we spoke, we talked through DWYWD. I said, "Assuming he stays the same for a while longer, what will you do about your needs and feelings?"

She decided to write him a short note about how she was feeling to see if he would do things differently when he was more aware. She thought telling him on paper instead of in person would allow him to be less defensive and more receptive. Next, she planned some evening routines to fill her time when he was busy. She also committed to reaching out to some other special people who showed her kindness and affection so she didn't feel the loneliness of his temporary neglect so acutely. While this didn't change him, it reduced her stress level greatly and spared their marriage the agitation of her demanding his change.

We are always left with a modicum of control in every relationship and situation. When we focus our efforts and creativity in the area where we have power to make a difference, we will be freed from decision fatigue and feelings of hopelessness or overwhelm. Think of areas in your life where you can decide what you will do.

Narrow Your Options

As you go about making bigger decisions, it can often be helpful to apply a process of elimination. If you have too many choices, narrow your selection down to your top three choices. You can do this by asking yourself which of these options lines up with your primary purpose. When you narrow the choices to three, your decision automatically becomes less cluttered and is determined more easily.

After you whittle down your options, ask yourself which choices you have enough resources to support (time, money, emotional energy, etc). If you have chosen a method such as the Five F's or Chasing Your Decision Down, run each alternative through your process.

A Second Opinion

The Bible says a wise man seeks many wise counselors.[7] If you have a few trusted friends or relatives who know you well and give sound advice, bounce ideas and choices off them when you are able.

From my personal experience, I would say not to ask too many people or you will end up with more choices and points of view than you had before you asked. This only muddles the process. Carefully choose the people who speak into your life when it comes to making big decisions. I have a few specific women in my life who are wise, able to be objective, and not afraid to speak the truth in love to me. I often call them after I have prayed through choices. The perspective they shed is invaluable.

Make This Chapter Mine:

After reading this chapter, what stands out that I want to remember?

How can I apply the kinds of rigorous questions to my decision making like the ones Greg McKeown suggests?

What do I want my go-to method(s) to be when it comes to big decisions?

Who are my go-to "wise counsellors"?

> The Lord is my strength and my shield;
> My heart trusted in Him, and I am helped;
> Therefore my heart greatly rejoices,
> And with my song I will praise Him.
> ~ Psalm 28:7

> *"One always has time enough,*
> *if one will apply it well."*
> — *Johann Wolfgang von Goethe.*

Chapter Twenty-Six
Life-Giving Habits

I started working as an independent contractor in my mid-twenties. In my youthful naivety, I thought I would easily transition from the world of time clocks and supervisors to autonomously managing my time and responsibilities.

Many evenings after his work day ended, my boyfriend (now husband) would ask if we could do something together. My way too frequent reply was that I still had work to finish. One day he commented that my transition to self-employment seemed to have loaded me with more than was good for me. I had to confess the truth. My mismanagement of each day's workload left me with a stack of catch-up by evening.

I tended to take longer lunches, allowed myself

to watch an occasional show on the Home Channel midday, and even worked in some exercise or cooking in the afternoon. Instead of being diligent to put first things first, I allowed the openness of my unmonitored work situation to foster a series of poor habits.

In a Rut

Face it. You and I already have habits. The question is whether the habits we have are the ones we want. How can we change our lives to include the habits we most want while eliminating those we don't?

When I began working independently from home, I didn't give habit formation a second thought. My failure to realize the patterns I was creating caused me to develop some routines with side effects that rippled into my personal life. Had I given this some forethought, I could have avoided the challenging work of undoing my bad habits in order to develop new ones.

Believe it or not, our brains are wired for habit. Not only do we have "ruts" in our brain, which function like marble runs – when a trigger goes off, we respond in a patterned way – but, we also have a part of the prefrontal cortex which holds onto any habit once it is formed.[1] This is both good and bad news.

When it comes to breaking habits, we are literally swimming upstream, attempting to create new ruts while convincing the stubborn part of our brain to let go and change. You can easily see how this makes breaking habits difficult.

Actually, breaking an old habit is far more difficult than beginning a new one. Knowing this brings up two key points. First of all, we need to adjust our expectations. Old habits don't die, they only go dormant, and getting them to sleep can be as difficult as settling a grumpy, overtired preschooler.

Secondly, knowing how hard it is to break old habits, we will do far better to start new, opposing habits than to try to eliminate our old, unhealthy ones. In other words, if you head to the freezer for a pint of Ben and Jerry's every time you are upset, instead of trying to stop emotional eating, you need to build in something new to do when you feel the trigger of being upset. Perhaps you pray, take a walk, or call a friend.

It's like a marble is sitting on top of a chute. The marble is you feeling upset. The chute is eating a tub of Chubby Hubby with whipped cream and chocolate sauce. You create a new chute of "pray and call a friend" and intentionally practice sending the marble down that chute. In time, with practice, you will start to notice your inclination change when you get upset.

The good news is once our brain has a new habit ingrained, we will keep at it with more ease over time. That same part of the brain that won't release bad habits, doesn't dismiss good ones either.

Choices Make Habits

Every small choice is like a drop of water in the bucket. Most of us give no heed to the drops as they compile. It's only when the bucket fills that we notice. Each drop contributed to the whole. Choices are like drops of water pooling to create habits. Every effort towards a goal matters. Each movement away also makes a difference.

C.S. Lewis wrote a poignant thought about the cumulative effect of our little choices:

Every time you make a choice you are

turning the central part of you, the part of you that chooses, into something a little different than it was before. And taking your life as a whole, with all your innumerable choices, all your life long you are slowly turning this central thing into a heavenly creature or a hellish creature: either into a creature that is in harmony with God, and with other creatures, and with itself, or else into one that is in a state of war and hatred with God, and with its fellow creatures, and with itself. To be the one kind of creature is heaven: that is, it is joy and peace and knowledge and power. To be the other means madness, horror, idiocy, rage, impotence, and eternal loneliness. Each of us at each moment is progressing to the one state of the other. [2]

Sin patterns don't come into our lives like an avalanche. Bad habits are built one choice, one action, one movement at a time. Life-giving habits develop in the same way.

Setting the Compass

When my husband and I owned a sailboat in our early marriage, we took it out several times on bigger trips to local islands. The compass had degrees by which we set our course. At a certain point in our voyage, we could no longer see the port we left, and we had no view yet of the destination. Around us water spread out to the horizon on all sides. We had to rely on that compass. One degree off and we would miss the island entirely. Like a compass, our daily choices must line up with our purpose or we will miss our desired destination.

In this chapter I want to share a few life-giving habits I have practiced for several years. I haven't merely thought about these or heard of them, I've done the work to make them part of how I live. They have freed up so much of my time and helped me efficiently get to the day-to-day needs of my home. I hope they do the same for you.

The Power of 20 Minutes

I'm not going to lie. Sometimes my desk looks like I won the mad professor award! No wood showing, only all those important pieces of paper sit stacked in random piles waiting for my attention ... and waiting ... and waiting.

Mostly this is because I'm not so much of a desk

person. I like to sit with my laptop (They call them that for a reason, right?) on our bed with a bunch of pillows behind me or to sprawl out on the couch with all sorts of books and supplies spread over every surrounding cushion. Still, I regularly need to get to that desk.

One day when I was procrastinating the massive chore of sorting, filing, reading, and tossing all those papers, it dawned on me that I didn't have to conquer this mountain in one fell swoop. I could break the task into bites and get through it in time. The 20-minute purge was born of necessity that day.

The 20-minute purge consists of me going in to my desk and picking up one pile of papers. I spend about 10 minutes sorting these papers into stacks of "to do," "to file," "to read," and "to toss." Then, I file and toss the ones in those piles for about five minutes.

I put the "to read" papers in a slot in my desk to get to at a designated time later that week. I set the "to do" papers neatly on the side of my desk and put times to get to those in my calendar for the week. Then I spend the last five minutes cleaning up any mess I have left.

I apply this 20-minute process to many different projects now. I can spend a short burst of time in the garden, thinning and responding to email, getting on social media with a focus, or doing a quick spot cleaning in our home.

I even use the 20 minute purge for going through our home on a regular basis. I may pick a closet or drawer and take everything out to sort for 10 minutes. Then I toss what's going to the trash, pile up what's being given away, and return the rest to the closet in the remaining 10 minutes.

Even if I don't finish the project of a whole closet in that time, I can organize a shelf or two. I can return a different day to spend another 20 minutes. We eat the elephant one bite at a time, and before we know it, we've gotten through something huge.

I've been to webinars on paper management for moms. The system presented would take a minor in organization to learn. I've also downloaded some super thick eBooks on how to set up an home management system. Most of these are stored unread on my hard drive! By using the uncomplicated 20-minute purge to clear my desk and complete other home tasks, I have learned to keep it simple and get it done.

The Pomodoro Method

Much like the 20-minute purge, Francesco Cirillo, an author and entrepreneur, developed a system in the 1990s called the Pomodoro Method (named after the tomato shaped kitchen timer he used).[3] The method employs short bursts of focus alternating with frequent breaks to accomplish tasks. In the Pomodoro Method time is used in 25 minute intervals (called Pomodoros) with a five minute break following each one. After every four Pomodoros you take a slightly longer break.

I renamed the Pomodoro for us moms. I call it the "Momodoro." It works well for the whole family. As we home educate, I can set a timer for 25 minutes and say, "Let's do math!" and then when time is up, I can send the boys out to jump on the trampoline.

The Momodoro applies in so many areas. Your family will get used to it if you use it consistently. I don't have the timer going all day long. That would be a bit to militant for me. I think I might feel like the timer had become the boss. We do use the timer to keep us on task for things we have to get through so we can be freed up for the activities we want to do without any awareness of time or deadlines.

We can do a clean sweep (tidying of the home) in 25 minutes and then take a five minute break to reward ourselves. If I need undivided time to myself, I can have my boys do something for 25 minutes and spend time filling their love tanks the five minutes before and after my Momodoro of alone time.

When Multitasking Works

Earlier on we said multitasking is a myth. It's true whenever brainpower is required, we cannot do more than one thing well simultaneously. As Greg McKeown says, there's a difference between multitasking and multi-focusing.[4] When it comes to tasks not requiring much thought, we can combine them for the sake of efficiency.

I have a treasured friendship with Amy. We both have full lives. Over the years we have found we have to be intentional about making time with one another. This year we started our Monday morning walk. By stacking friend time and exercise, we are doing double duty.

The same goes when I listen to a podcast while I'm on the gym treadmill or call my mom while I'm washing dishes. I sometimes bring my current writing project to the boys' play rehearsal or piano practice. When the body is doing something redundant, the brain can engage in something else. This is positive and effective multitasking, and it frees up time in other parts of our week.

After reading this chapter, what stands out that I want to remember?

What habits do I have that I would like to replace with healthier choices?

How can the Momodoro or 20-minute purge help me get to what needs to be done?

What can I multitask to get done more efficiently?

"All things are lawful for me,"
but not all things are helpful.
"All things are lawful for me,"
but I will not be enslaved by anything.
1 Corinthians 6:12

*"It is really essential for your well-being
to regulate your life and habits
in a sensible way."*
~ Eleanor Roosevelt

Chapter Twenty-Seven
Cementing Your Habits

I want to talk about the ways we can build in habits that stick. The last thing I want is for you to read this book and never implement the good ideas you find here or to try the ideas on for a hot minute when you are inspired and then abandon your efforts as quickly as you began.

Habit Stacking

In his book *Habit Stacking*, S. J. Scott shares how it is possible to make dozens of small changes by building them into a new routine.[1] Instead of trying to change a whole bunch of things at once, we can create a single routine which contains a series of smaller actions linked together.

Crystal Paine of Money Saving Mom has created

two courses aimed at supporting the concept of building routine in a practical way: *Make Over Your Mornings* and *Make Over Your Evenings*. In her courses Crystal walks moms through a series of lessons addressing habits to build into each segment of the day accordingly.

Another way to stack habits without revamping your whole routine is to attach a new habit to be formed to an existing, established habit. Your current habits are already locked in place in your life and brain. By tacking a desired habit before or after something you already do by rote, you string it so your brain begins to associate the new habit with the old one.

I did this last year when I wanted to incorporate making my bed into my morning routine. I have taught my boys to make their beds but always justified leaving mine a mess because I'm the mom, and my life is too full for superfluous chores. One day I decided I like the look of a made bed. A graduation speech given by a Navy Seal about the way making your bed sets your day off to a good start[2] solidified my motivation.

I always take my thyroid medication first thing in the morning, then put on my glasses and

Fitbit. I decided I would stack the habit of making my bed right after these three existing parts of my routine. Every day when I finished fastening the Fitbit to my wrist, I would turn back to my bedroom and make my bed. I now do this without a thought. As a matter of fact, it takes a lot to get me to leave my bed undone.

To start stacking habits, you might want to make a list of your existing day-to-day habits. Then make a list of habits you would like to incorporate into your life. Rate those habits as to which ones are most to least important or valuable. Take the top one and stack it somewhere before or after an existing habit. Practice it until it is solidified, then go back to your list and pick the next one.

Process, Not Outcome

As we think about habit formation we often want to do it all, and right away. We need to make realistic goals and then work slowly and consistently to strengthen the habits that lead towards the goals we set. Perfectionism kills habits before they have a chance to start forming. When you fall off your new habit, simply dust yourself off and start up again. It really is that simple.

Anne Bogel of Modern Mrs. Darcy shared how she has learned to implement goals that work: "I focus on the process which I can control, not the outcome, which I cannot."[3] Brilliant. As we put new habits in place, we need to take Anne's wisdom to heart. We can celebrate the goodness of going to the gym rather than berating ourselves for not losing another pound.

Cheerleaders and Coaches

Finally, most successful habits happen in a community of support. It may be as simple as asking your best friend to support you as you take on your new behavior bit by bit. On the other hand, you may need to get more formal in how you elicit encouragement.

After years of trying to lose weight and improve my physical fitness, my husband and I decided to dedicate a portion of our budget to a personal trainer. We sat down to count the cost, and I hired a young man at our gym for six months. I can't tell you how many weeks I would have stopped going or diminished my effort if visions of Micael hadn't danced through my head. Whatever it takes, build in the support you need to make your habits become a reality.

The Transition

The two different births of my boys were as opposite as their personalities. My oldest son came into the world after 48 hours of hard labor, followed by an emergency C-Section. My second son, due to the complications in my first labor, was born via scheduled C-Section.

I will say, mothering these two boys has followed this pattern. One seems to need a lot of effort on my part, yet is so worth all the strain I go through to mother him well. The other is a more easy-going personality.

One thing I know about labor, right when things get difficult, we transition. This stage of labor involves lots of pain without much to show for it. Medical commentaries about transition note that a woman is often inconsolable and irritable during this part of the birth process.[4]

The birthing of a habit seems to go along in a similar way. We labor and work hard. It can hurt to let go of what we were doing and put something new in place. When we most want results, our habit practice can hit the wall, delivering very little in terms of what we would call progress.

Another way to think about this is the transition we experience when we come off a merry-go-round. Things are still spinning for a while, and we need to adjust to the slower pace. Adopting a healthier rhythm of life means stepping off the whirl of our old ways.

Give yourself time to transition into new habits. Don't expect miracles unless you know the miracle must be followed by a time to solidify the gifts it brought. We don't change overnight. We have to adjust, acclimate, modify, and continue to grow.

In time, we actually become more fruitful and productive because functioning without adrenaline and stress makes the brain work more optimally.

The free resources available on my website to accompany this book are designed to give you tools to help you in this process. You might also consider going through this book with a group of women to help one another grow in knowing your purpose, making room for what matters most, and solidifying habits you desire to incorporate in your lives.

I don't want you to put down this book, give me a five-star rating on Amazon (though you are welcome to do that!) and think back in a month wondering what you read that moved you so much. I deeply care that you take these principles and practices and make them yours. I hope you walk away from this book making life changes that bless you and those you love.

Dance Like Nobody's Watching

Sometimes slowing feels lonely, empty, or fruitless. We may come face to face with our need to perform for approval. The rest of our friends and family may not embrace a slowed down lifestyle.

At several points in my journey when I committed to doing less, I experienced the gap between what I chose and the way many of my dear friends were living. They were still attending all the things, seeing one another regularly, and keeping full, busy schedules. I was home more often than not. It felt a bit like I had cut myself off and become a hermit for no good reason. I had to endure that feeling, reminding myself the reasons I needed to pull back including putting an end to the nutty level of overactivity I had decided to trade for a more meaningful lifestyle.

As we realign our priorities, we walk through some loss. Every gain has sacrifices attached to it. Remember, you are choosing what is best. That means letting go of a lot of what may be good, but is not good for you.

Going the Distance

My friends who run marathons don't just get up one morning and run 26 miles. In order to be in the condition they need to be to run that long distance, they train by running shorter distances and then adding longer distances over time. We have to approach intentional living like a marathon. New skills that we put in place need our regular attention.

Over time if we allow ourselves to go on without intentionally implementing the skills we learn here, we will lose them. Suddenly we will wonder how we got so busy again with all the clutter piled up everywhere. The bottom line is living on purpose requires cultivating habits that work for us. Then we need to continually work to maintain those like a marathon runner maintains her skill at long-distance running.

<u>Make This Chapter Mine:</u>

After reading this chapter, what stands out that I want to remember?

How can I stack habits to routines and habits I already have in place?

How can I invite "cheerleaders" to support a new habit I am cultivating?

How does knowing there will be a transition help me prepare as I put new habits in place?

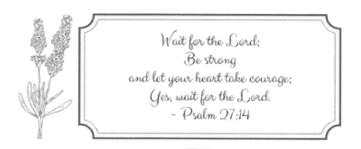

Wait for the Lord;
Be strong
and let your heart take courage;
Yes, wait for the Lord.
~ Psalm 27:14

"One always has time enough,
if one will apply it well."
— Johann Wolfgang von Goethe.

Chapter Twenty-Eight
What Keeps Us Bound

If you call America home, you live immersed in a culture obsessed with more. We want more money, more things, more activities, more followers on social media. We live in a dissatisfied society with an insatiable craving for the next new thing.

The Evolution of Expansion

In 1950 the average home size was 1,065 square feet according to a Harvard report.[1] When I was growing up in the 1970s, it was normal for children to share a bedroom with at least one of their siblings. Looking at Forbes in 2017, the average home size had grown to 2,500 square feet.[2] We not only take up more space, but we own more stuff. Many families rent storage to pack away unused things.

Filling Spaces

Does any of this add to our happiness? Some of it truly does. I have some possessions that bring me joy: our piano when either of my sons sits playing, a few decorative items placed throughout the living room and kitchen to make our home feel welcoming and personally ours. The patio furniture out back which I paid for with money I earned from leading a retreat. We linger there and connect as a family, or friends visit to chat over tea as we pour our hearts out and share laughter.

So much of what we own, though, is mere stuff. It fills our houses and our time with needs to repair, to store, and to clean. Our stuff doesn't simply take up physical space, it takes up psychological space. This is why I have become a huge fan of the regular practice of purging.

Room to Breathe

I can't remember when I took up the habit of purging. I know it was before the birth of my first-born who is almost 17 now. It may have started with our move to a new home.

My faithful friends and I stood at my dining

table, my six-month pregnant belly protruding, sorting and wrapping shells and candles for hours. Shells and candles. Was I opening a shop? No. I simply hoarded these things to the tune of four under the bed boxes full. The irony came as we toted those boxes to storage in the middle of July. I had my own wax museum when we opened them the following February.

That experience, along with the nesting hormones of pregnancy, sparked the urge to purge. You may think it was smooth sailing from then on. Wouldn't it be awesome if I never bought another useless item, overstocked on candles, or filled my closets with clothing I never wore? Like all skills, purging has come over time with all the learning curves you might expect.

One year I heard a gal share about her practice of annually purging before the school year started. Sounded good to me. Another year I read something about the November habit of gratitude. To cultivate thankfulness, each member of the family rids themselves of one item a day. It could be some junk in their room they take to the kitchen trash can. More significantly it might be an item they know someone else could find more useful, so they bring it out to be donated. Our family incorporated this practice every year.

Do the math. With four of us and 30 days in the month, we clear out 120 items every November (just in time to reload at Christmas. Ah, the beauty of Western culture!). We don't usually regain the whole whopping 120, so we're still ahead by the time the New Year's Ball drops in Times Square.

I decided to integrate one more annual purge. Being a fan of spring cleaning, I put a regular household purge on the family calendar for March. If you are tracking with me, we have routine purges in March, August, and November.

Clinging and Releasing

With all this ridding of unnecessary stuff, you may picture us each owning one fork, spoon, knife, and plate, and having just enough clothing to make it through a week. Not by a longshot. Somehow we still manage to have more than we need, and often more than we want.

If you think this is a problem only wealthy families face, it just isn't so. We are about as middle class as they come. Drive through neighborhoods where less affluent families live, and you will see clutter in yards including old playsets, broken washing machines, ripped plastic pools, and other what-nots all over the property. We simply cling to stuff way beyond its usefulness.

I've observed one more phenomenon through the years as I continue to perfect the purge. Somehow I manage to allow certain things to pass by my scrutiny. Later, during the next purge, as I re-encounter an item I had kept, I wonder how it made it under the radar and past the donation bag last time. I'm usually more willing to let it go at that point than I was four or five months prior.

I'm getting more ruthless over the years. Still, either sentimentality or fear that we will need something and not have it can cause clinging when it would be far more beneficial to bid an item adieu.

Repeated purging is a blessing. We become more used to saying "farewell" the more regularly we practice donating and throwing away what isn't needed. Ridding ourselves of surplus teaches us what really matters. We learn how sweet it feels to give to others and to release the weight of all the things clogging up our homes and hearts. We treasure what we choose to keep, and we are freed of the burden of what goes.

Purging Questions to Ask

When it comes to purging, I've refined my methods and approaches over the years. One of the best tools I've found is to ask myself three simple questions.

- Is it purposeful? (Do we use it?)
- Is it meaningful? (Will my grandkids want this in 50 years?)
- Is it beautiful? (Does it define home and create the welcome we want to exude to one another and guests?)

Greg McKeown gets all ninja when it comes to purging. In the book *Essentialism*, which you have heard me refer to repeatedly, he says we need to detach ourselves from a sense of ownership. When we step back and view an item as though it were not ours, we can ask ourselves what we would pay or do to acquire it. Do we absolutely love this item? [3] Oh dear. That eliminates about two thirds of my current post-purge possessions.

Call a Friend

It's awesome to purge with others. The accountability and support we gain knowing others are going through the same process of releasing possessions spurs us on. We may need the nudge to let go at times when we can't quite make that final cut.

You may have seen various bloggers host purging challenges. People join together by posting images of what they are clearing out on Instagram with a common hashtag. Sometimes I've texted or talked with a few friends, and we've started our own purges simultaneously. We text one another pictures and spur one another on towards being more mindful of what fills our homes.

I have also taken numerous pictures of myself in various clothing items, texted these to a friend, and asked, "Keep or toss?" Her feedback gave me the impetus to pass on some things I would have otherwise stored one more year. When I truly can't release a clothing item, I put a rubber band at the top of the hanger. If I haven't worn that by the time the next purge comes around, out it goes.

Sentimental Stuff

Purging isn't always as easy as it seems it would be. We attach emotions to our possessions. Letting them go can spark a moment of grief. After that passes, we feel either relief or contentment. Sometimes I've had to let go of things and in the process say "goodbye" to a dream that went along with them.

I'm not ever going to hand stamp cards the way I did before I had children. I don't need a craft-store aisle full of rubber stamps waiting for me under the guest bed "just in case" I start this up again. Still, releasing those stamps to someone else caused me to admit that season had come to a close for me. I have other hobbies and callings. I need to make room for those.

A Legacy of Release

One of the greatest byproducts of purging consistently has been the impact it has had on my boys. When my older son was in elementary school, he liked to keep many of his creations.

As he has aged, he has been more prone to want simplicity and a minimalist surrounding. It suits him.

My younger son is very sentimental. Everything holds a special place in his heart and has deep meaning to him. As we have continued to practice purging as a family, I have watched him learn to let go and acquire the capacity to discern whether something is truly valuable or can be given away. I've witnessed both the boys becoming more sensitive to the needs of others. As we purge, they may say something like, "Mom, I think someone else would use this more than I do."

Our practice as a family has made us less attached to things in general. We love the things most precious to us, but that list is short and far less valuable than our "to love" list. Just writing this makes me want to put down the laptop and start purging. I hope it has the same effect on you.

<u>*Make This Chapter Mine:*</u>

After reading this chapter, what stands out that I want to remember?

Do I cling to things I could release?

What are my barriers to letting go?

Which purging habit Patty mentioned best fits our family? How can I implement it?

Do not store up for yourselves
treasures on earth ...
But store up for yourselves treasures in heaven
For where your treasure is,
there your heart will be also.
~ Matthew 6: 19-21

"An empty lantern provides no light.
Self-care is the fuel that allows
your light to shine brightly."
~ Unknown

Chapter Twenty-Nine
Self-Care Isn't Always Selfish

Here I go, jumping into the fire! The topic of self-care often becomes controversial. A dear friend once said, "I keep hearing all these women talk about self-care. We need to spend more time thinking of others than ourselves. This self-care movement seems so selfish."

Before we toss her thoughts completely aside, I want to share my own journey in this area. When I was a young mom, I took stock of many other moms I knew. We do that. Sometimes it's not in the best spirit. Often, it's simply to get a clue on this thing called motherhood. We observe other moms wondering, "How are you managing this?" or "What works well?"

As I watched, I noticed certain moms spent an

inordinate amount of time volunteering at church, being in run clubs that met at the local bagel shop at 4:30am several mornings a week, going to the gym, and getting their nails done. I noted that the children of these moms sometimes seemed to have more quality time with childcare workers than with their own mothers.

Judge and Jury

I judged. I'm not proud of it, but I did. Instead of realizing we're all doing the best we can, I determined I wasn't going to be like "those" moms. My boys were going to have as much of me as they could. Besides the days I worked out of town (Oh, that's different, don't you know?), I was going to be by their side and invested in their lives.

My decision meant shunning all self-care and defining it as self-indulgent. I didn't exercise if it meant taking time away from my boys. I only served in ministry where they could be with me. I took them into the inner city, wore my infant on my body while teaching VBS, and brought my child into Bible Study instead of leaving him in the nursery. The pendulum swung the other way. You may have heard it said, "One-hundred-and-eighty degrees of sick is sick."

Just to be clear, calling a sitter and taking time to get a pedicure, or getting up early to run with other moms are both wonderful things to add into your routine. I was wrong to judge other moms for taking care of themselves. The problem comes when our children spend an excessive amount of their life in childcare all so mom can have some "me-time." Too much "self-care" *is* self-indulgent.

There is a way, though, to incorporate your own needs into the rhythm of your family life while still maintaining a very strong presence to meet the needs of your people. As a matter of fact, being filled makes us more able to be attentive and to have the best us to offer to those we love most.

Learning Self-Care

As I have matured and grown in trust, God has brought me away from a spirit of condemnation and fear. Somehow, He simultaneously taught me the value of self-care. I no longer judge other moms. I realize we are all doing our level best.

In my life, increasing self-care has included regularly going to the gym and eating relatively well. My week includes adequate sleep every night. I even budget in pedicures or a massage every once in a while.

Growing into self-care has been just as wonky as every other kind of growth I've experienced in life. I started with a rigid approach towards building in activities to nourish my body and soul. Over time I have learned to ask myself what would fill my tank. Then I'm sure to add a life-giving activity to my day or week.

During a season of stress and grief, one of my wisest friends, Kathy, spoke consistently to me about self-care. I'm not kidding you when I say we barely had a phone conversation that didn't include a loving admonishment to take care of myself.

Mom-Care

On an already full work day when I needed to head to Los Angeles for client meetings, a situation with my teen flared up. Instead of getting on the road ahead of schedule, I spent the first few hours of my day in the school counselor's office and on follow up phone calls resolving details.

This incident followed a few stressful weeks. It was the proverbial straw that broke this camel's back. I didn't know how deeply the pressure had been impacting me until I started experiencing a growing headache throughout the day, accompanied by a sense of nausea. As my meetings progressed, I felt worse.

After work I travelled 45 minutes to have a scheduled visit with my mentor. We met at her home and drove to a little Asian restaurant nearby. My headache continued to spread and worsen. I began feeling dizzy. I tried to eat but couldn't. I finally told her what I was experiencing. We took our food to go and returned to her home.

She set me up in her guest bed, gave me some Tylenol, and turned down the lights. I tossed a bit from the tremendous pain in my head, but finally settled to a deep sleep.

When I awoke, she was gently touching my shoulder, telling me she had contacted my husband for my medical information. She asked if I needed to go to the hospital. I actually felt surprisingly improved. Her husband had made "stoup" (a soup-like stew). She brought me a set of cozy pajamas and asked if I thought I could eat. I gratefully ate and relaxed in their caring presence. I called my husband, brushed my teeth, and went back to sleep.

The following morning, I woke at 5:30am. I found her already sitting at the kitchen table reading her devotion. She offered me breakfast, and we sat eating overlooking their garden out the window.

I wish I could bottle the sweetness of their care. I had lost sight of my need for filling during the weeks of stress leading up to this physical collapse. My body screamed out for what my soul missed. I raced through "yield" and "stop" signs and paid the ticket in the form of a raging migraine.

In God's mercy, my mentor and her husband provided me a place of refuge. I didn't need to think, prepare, plan, or execute anything. I could simply rest and receive. My deepest need for care was provided at last.

On many occasions in the year following that migraine as our family experienced several traumatic experiences in succession, I would lay my head on my own pillow at home at night but imagine I was in my mentor's home, in those sweet pajamas, without a care in the world. I could coax myself to fall into a sound sleep by recalling the gentle safety of their home.

All Goodness Comes from Fullness

In John 15, Jesus shares a story about God being like a vine and us being the branches.[1] He invites us to abide in His love. I often share an object lesson when I lead women's retreats related to this story. I set a cup on a saucer. Under the saucer is a salad plate. The bottom of the pile has a dinner plate.

I hold a pitcher full of water over this stack and begin pouring into the cup. While I do, I explain:

> "This pitcher is like God, and the water is His love. Imagine there is an infinite supply. As He pours into you, all you need to do is be still and receive.
>
> The love you gain from abiding in Him starts to automatically flow onto the people immediately around you. Then the love goes out into your community and the world. All we do is allow God to fill us. From this filling,

we pour out."

Have you ever tried serving when your bucket was completely empty, and you were feeling disconnected from God? You end up more burnt out and resentful. We cannot pour from an empty cup. We must allow time to be filled.

Motherhood is 24-7. We can become depleted from all the varying demands of our children, husband, home, and other commitments. When everyone needs us, it seems impossible to step back and carve out time for self-care. If we don't, we are trying to fill others' cups without anything in our own. I encourage you as I remind myself – we have to take time to be filled so we can pour goodness from our fullness into the lives of our family, friends, community, and the world.

Owning our Self-Care

Perhaps as we look back over our childhood, we feel resentful that our parents didn't do a good job of meeting our deepest needs as children. While it is often helpful to process the feelings left over from the past, clinging to resentment doesn't help us as adults.

I've learned that no one is going to come knocking trying to make sure my needs are met, and my tank is full. (Well, occasionally Amy shows up with a muffin and my favorite latte for no reason whatsoever; Jenn will unexpectedly send me Scripture in a text; or Kathy will message me asking, "How are you doing today?") Let's just put it this way: no one is going to top their daily to-do list with "Meet Patty's Needs." As adults, we superintend the filling of our own tanks. That means asking for what we require and making space for our needs to be met within the whole picture of life.

How Do You Care for You?

Self-care can look different for each of us. If you are an introvert, you may need time alone. This is no joke. I encourage my introverted friends to carve out times of solitude by asking their husbands or extended family to pitch in to care for their children. If you are a single mom or your husband isn't available to support you in this way, save somewhere in your budget to pay a sitter or trade times of childcare with a friend.

If you are an extrovert, you may need to build in some time having fun with friends. Kid-free time with other adults can fill your tank and give you the boost you need so you can return to motherhood with new energy and perspective.

When I asked moms to tell me what they do to care for themselves, I sometimes got blank stares or a laugh. Other moms did say that they have cultivated hobbies such as taking a painting class, riding their bike, or gardening. Some women told me spending time alone in prayer and the Word refreshed them more than anything else. They had learned the beauty of approaching time with God as a place of rest rather than a task to complete.

If you aren't sure what self-care looks like for you, try some things out. Taking a little midday rest might be a good start. If you don't have the slightest clue as to what might be a self-care activity for you, ask yourself what you would do if you had a day off? Think back to things you really enjoyed as a child. Did you love music, art, dance? Does being outdoors fill you? What about going to museums, reading, or even simply napping. Try things on.

Another way to do this is to ask yourself what you would do for you if you were a friend of yours. If you imagine a friend caring for you, what would they do? Taking an objective view of ourselves can help us see what we really crave in terms of care.

No Goals, Only Care

When we are uber-busy, we don't get to explore fun as much as we might like. Everything is a to-do. We rush through and accomplish all things. Even gatherings with friends are overshadowed by clouds of preparation and thoughts of "what's next." To truly care for ourselves, we have to remove an emphasis on goals and evaluation.

If exercise fills your tank, that's awesome. As soon as it becomes about losing that last five pounds, you have turned this into a chore instead of a delight. Goal-orientation invites the future into the present, and keeps us from savoring the experience for what it is. You know I'm all about goal setting and living on purpose. That said, we need to learn to separate the goal from the activity once we are engaged in it.

I attend a Hip-Hop class, a Zumba class, and a crazy difficult Barre class each week. I love those exercise classes. I dig in and dance my heart out or focus and follow the moves. I choose those particular classes because I love taking them regardless of whether I lose weight or not. Let your filling and self-care be a source of pleasure to you. That way you will enjoy the process rather than only appreciating the outcome.

<u>Make This Chapter Mine:</u>

After reading this chapter, what stands out that I want to remember?

Where am I on the spectrum of self-care? Do I chafe at it, or am I prone to overindulge in it?

What could healthy self-care look like for me?

How can I ensure my cup is filled?

Do you not know that your bodies are temples
of the Holy Spirit, who is in you,
whom you have received from God?
You are not your own; ...
Therefore honor God with your bodies.
~ 1 Corinthians 6: 19-20

"Generosity isn't an act. It's a way of life."
~ Chip Ingram

Chapter Thirty

Give A Little

Families tend to tell certain stories about different members through the years. My family lore includes a childhood story of me voluntarily emptying my piggy bank to give to the Red Cross after a tornado decimated a nearby town. Even though I naturally jump in when I see a need, my giving hasn't always been rooted in the healthiest motives.

I have shared with you many of the ways I gave from broken and empty places inside me. The more I have allowed healing, which has taken time, courage, and the gracious hand of God, the more I have been able to give from the fullness and overflow of my heart. Like the cup overflowing onto the saucer, my abiding relationship with God has given me abundance in my heart to spill onto people around me.

Blessed to Be a Blessing

It can be easy to approach giving with a burden to serve others. From this stance, we make giving into a law rather than a privilege and natural result of God's love in us. Serving from a sense of obligation can burn you out faster than a cheap firecracker.

I looked up the word *generosity*, and found out it comes from a Latin root, *generosus* which means *of noble birth*. Over the years the word came to mean *having a quality of nobility*, and then *the virtue of giving good things to others freely and abundantly*. In order to give our time and resources freely, we need to be unattached to them. Knowing we have all we need, we freely give from the overflow of what our generous God provides to us.

Getting Out of My Own Way

I don't know about you, but my mind can spiral inward, and I can become self-focused with thoughts about my day and the things concerning me. One of the most obvious benefits of giving has been that I am taken out of myself. When I give to other people, my mind lifts to include thoughts of others.

Self-centeredness is a trap. Giving opens the snare of self and allows me to experience joy and freedom as I consider other people and their needs.

Giving also allows me to partner with God in blessing those He loves. He allows me to reflect His gracious and thoughtful nature as I consider others' needs and share what I have to bless them. As I emulate Him, He causes me to grow to be more like Him.

Leaving the Perimeter Available

The Old Testament contains numerous accounts where God commands His people to leave a perimeter of their crops unpicked for the foreigner and poor among them. The remnant provided for the needs of people who had no other means of gathering food.

Recently I have been thinking about the amount of time we have to spend in our lives.   What if we viewed it like an Israelite's crop? As we create margin (not grabbing every minute up for ourselves or packing our schedules to the brim), we open space for others to lay claim to our time as well. Can we leave the edges of our lives for those who might need us and what we offer?

Giving our time can be like tithing. When we tithe our money, we acknowledge God as the owner of all our resources. We give a tenth or more of our money and come to discover we have plenty left in the 90% that remains. Stepping out in faith cultivates and confirms our belief in God's abundant provision.

Time is not money, contrary to the popular saying. We could always obtain more money. Our time is numbered and finite. Still, the principle of tithing in either of these resources brings the same outcome. When we set aside a portion of our time to intentionally serve and bless others, we find we have been given enough time to do all we have been called to do.

When we realize we have enough time, we aren't as stingy with it. We don't need to be anxious. Living a life consisting of a rhythm of planning, resting, and leaving margin helps us save the edges of our lives for unexpected needs God wants to fill through us. I have found the greatest fulfillment and joy by trusting God as I give of my time to others.

Do Drop In

I grew up in the Midwest. I clearly remember

people popping by for no reason and without forewarning. When I was 20 years old, I relocated to California where people live according to their calendars. When I want to spend time with a friend, it is the custom to call or text, and then to make a plan for a few weeks out. This lack of spontaneous connecting has been a huge adjustment for me. Even after 30 years of living in this state, I find myself missing the sweetness of unexpected visits in the middle of a day.

One morning, as I was puttering around the house getting a few things done, a woman I mentor showed up to the door. We had gotten our wires crossed and she thought it was the day and time we had set to meet. I didn't have anything pressing, so I invited her in. We sat together talking about a situation in her life. Within a few minutes tears formed in her eyes. She shared a deep burden as I listened, spoke encouragement, and then prayed with her.

Had this happened in the days when I was packing my schedule so full I couldn't breathe, I would have missed the opportunity to be present for her. The margin around my life was hers that day.

Pausing to be Present

Giving our undivided presence to someone shows our care in immeasurable ways. Children need our time and attention more than they often let on. Sometimes, my younger son asks me to bake muffins or make a smoothie with him. The neighborhood boys might coax me to stop what I'm doing so I can watch them do tricks on their bikes out front. As small as these requests may seem, setting aside my agenda to invest in the children around me is a gift to them and a blessing to me.

We have a family friend whose health has declined. She depends on oxygen now. She rarely takes trips out of the home. One afternoon the boys and I set aside what we were doing to pop in and catch up with her. Not only did this visit make a difference to her, it sent a message to my boys. We make room to care for others.

When life is overly packed and busy, thinking about special people might be last on our list. We zoom from commitment to obligation without a pause button. Building in margin with the intention of giving to others creates room to truly be with other people in meaningful ways. Intentionally underfilling our schedule leaves the margin from which we can give our greatest gift – our undivided presence.

The Gift of Prayer

I recently visited a friend of mine who lives in another city. I had the privilege of going to a Bible study with the women in her group. They had been praying for our family over the few months prior to this visit while we were going through a challenging season.

At the end of the study, one woman approached me and specifically asked how our family was doing. I can't express the depth of gratitude I felt. Her thoughtfulness to remember our situation and ask me about it overwhelmed me. She gave me immeasurable gifts through her prayer and concern.

Prayer for others costs us a little time and energy. It means committing to care for someone by bringing them and whatever needs they are experiencing to God. As we pray for

others, we give a gift they may or may not come to know about. Because of this, we need to be careful about how often we tell others we are going to pray for them.

So many times people say, "I'll be praying for you." They may mean well but never remember to actually follow through. I have learned to carefully say, "I will be praying for you this week," or "I will pray for you today." I know I will be able to fulfill those commitments. Even better, if we are talking and a concern comes up, I offer prayer in the moment while we are together. Then, if God brings them to mind later, I pause and pray for them again.

Offering a Sacrifice

Offerings of our time can feel like sacrifices. Often giving costs us something. Giving cost Jesus everything. As we live for Him, we give to others as a spiritual act of worship and gratitude.

In the end God takes anything we give and returns it to us with blessings we couldn't imagine. We can't out-give God. The more we spend our life investing in others from healthy motives in our hearts, the more we experience joy and purpose.

God intends us to hold all things loosely so we can cling to Him alone. Sacrificial giving allows us to open our hands to others, and in the process, we learn to lean on God to provide our needs. As we pour into others, we depend on Him to provide what they need. We grow in releasing as we serve from a heart of love.

Growing in Giving

I believe I have a long way to go in this practice of living a life marked by generosity. I don't say this as a way to deprecate myself or measure giving as though it were a work to earn God's blessing. As I think through leaving the edges of my life open to others, I realize God is calling me to make openhandedness and focusing on others increasingly a way of life. To do this, I simply need to plan well, include rest in my plan so I can be filled, and then allow God to spill out on others from the overflow of my heart. Like all other character development, generosity grows with intention and practice.

Make This Chapter Mine:

After reading this chapter, what stands out that I want to remember?

How do I leave margin so I can bless others?

Have I tried to give from unhealthy motives?

What is God leading me towards in terms of how I use my time to bless others?

Each one must give
as he has decided in his heart,
not reluctantly or under compulsion,
for God loves a cheerful giver.
~ 2 Corinthians 9:7

*"If you are going to live, leave a legacy.
Leave a mark on the world
that can't be erased."*
~ Maya Angelou

Chapter Thirty-One
Your Lifetime Legacy

A few years ago during the winter, I was battling a cold. I woke in the middle of the night to get a dose of homeopathy to quell the hacking cough so I could sleep. As I approached the counter, a feeling of dizziness overwhelmed me. I staggered toward the living room and let out what sounded like a yelp as I fell.

The next thing I knew, I was on my back with my husband kneeling over me. My youngest son was standing near the wall of the kitchen staring at me with a look of both fear and relief on his face. My husband explained that he heard a noise and woke. When he came to the living room, he found me on my back, not breathing, with my eyes wide open. He had been a lifeguard in his teenage years, so CPR was second nature to him. He resuscitated me and, as I say, saved my life. (He won't take that credit, though we both know it's true.)

Why Am I Here?

One thing I clearly remember as the haze of the experience dissipated. Laying on my carpet at some time after 3:00am I had the thought: "There is much more to do." I considered all the ministry and care I wanted to extend. I had more words to write, and hopefully, more lives to touch.

It's cliché to say we are living on borrowed time. Truly, life is shorter than we imagine. Simply acknowledging the brevity of life can cause us to think thoughts like the Psalmist:

> *This is the day which the Lord has made.*
> *I will rejoice and be glad in it.* [1]

We have been given the day at hand, and are promised nothing else on earth. From this vantage point, every moment becomes smattered with sacred significance. Will we forget this precious truth? Yes. Spiritual amnesia blots it out repeatedly. It takes continually reminding ourselves of the sweet brevity of our sojourn here to keep us alert to living intentionally.

The life I have been given does not always feel amazing. Some days stink worse than a dog who just encountered a family of skunks: bad stuff. I've come to believe the trials of life give unspeakable gifts I couldn't obtain any other way. Following each storm I gain a clarity of focus and am more fully dependent upon God due to the way the difficulty taught me to lean on Him.

Purpose for the Duration

God made each of us for a purpose. That night in my living room, in a matter of moments, the poignant awareness of what matters most crystalized.

The year after that near-death experience, I turned 50 years old. I describe my midlife transition as a lifequake. The strangest sensation passed through me as I processed this milestone. My life was more than half over. I spent a few weeks absorbing what I had done so far with my life, and I received a renewed perspective as to what I wanted to do with the remaining years.

Spend It Well

If someone gave you $780,000 to spend and invest, you might squander a bit of it. As you got down to under $400,000 left, it's possible you would look at all you have spent, realizing how quickly it went. The remaining amount would gain value because it was all you had left.

Did you know that 90 years are comprised of about 780,000 hours? By age 50, I had used up 433,300. Some I've spent, some I've wasted terribly. What about the remainder? That's the key. When I consider life in terms of hours left to invest, each moment takes on greater significance.

None of us are guaranteed our life will last into our 90s. We live assuming our days will go on forever. When we take the perspective of someone on borrowed time, we learn to choose more wisely, selecting what matters most and letting many petty things go with ease.

As we close out this book, I want to ask you some of the hardest questions. Right here, I want to push you to really think about what you want your life to be most devoted to doing.

Who are your people to love? What has God made you to do that only you can uniquely complete? What character are you developing in yourself? Where will you spend these precious years, days, and moments of the life you have been given?

Will you be glad when you reflect back on your life, saying something like, "The kitchen was always spotless, and we were the best dressed family in the church directory," or "I had more Instagram followers than I had hoped."? If not, let's rearrange the priorities a tad.

This isn't about guilting yourself into making the best choices. No matter how intentional we are about living on purpose and slowing down for what matters most, we will experience some harried days and missed moments. Even after reading and applying all we have talked through, we will occasionally miss the mark.

Life is a glorious, limited gift. We can unwrap it and savor the goodness, or we can waste it on all the wrong things, zooming along without purpose and missing what matters most.

Considering Your Legacy

Ironically, the more awareness I have gained of

my own mortality, the more alive I have become. I find myself investing my time rather than squandering it. I think about whether I am living a life I want others to emulate, especially my children.

About four years ago, my friend, Amy, who is an estate attorney, was asked to speak at a MOPS group. I decided to surprise her by showing up at the talk to support her. She spoke on the need for each of us to have a will in place. Her talk encouraged moms to think carefully about what they were leaving their children. She had seen estates poorly planned and witnessed all the emotional and financial havoc resulting from this neglect.

I would venture to say our life's legacy extends beyond our will. Pondering the brevity of life leads us to think about how we want to be remembered by those who are closest to us. What critical lessons and values do we intend to pass on to our children? More importantly, what example will we leave them to follow?

As you close out this book, I hope you have gotten a better sense of your purpose and are beginning to pursue it, no matter how falteringly. I pray you are integrating more rest and addressing the root issues behind your own busyness. Maybe you are laying down perfectionism and embracing the wonky, wobbly road of extending grace towards yourself and others. Perhaps you are setting healthier boundaries and leaving greater margin.

I still wish we could sit on that back porch of mine, sipping a cup of cold tea or a mug of hot cocoa while you share your thoughts and all that is stirring within your heart about slowing and living for what matters most. After sharing this book with you, my desire would be to hear what you took away and how you are choosing differently than when you first cracked open the cover.

I hope you embrace the holy hidden in the ordinary, and honor God through your everyday, simple choices to slow and be present. Become the person you long to be. Love the people who matter most to you. Serve from the overflow of your heart. Find your purpose and clear the decks to make room for what matters most.

<u>Make This Chapter Mine:</u>

After reading this chapter, what stands out that I want to remember?

What legacy am I leaving my children?

Does my life model the things I value most?

If I can think of one way I can adjust how I am living to leave an example for those I love most, what will I change?

The life of mortals is like grass,
they flourish like a flower of the field;
the wind blows over it and it is gone,
and its place remembers it no more.
~ Psalm 103: 14-16

A Closing Prayer:

I want to close this book with a prayer for you as you slow down to live more intentionally:

Dear God,

You have given us the gift of life. You planned our days and numbered them. You know our hearts and what challenges us. Thank you that you are with us as we move towards a life with greater intention and purpose.

We confess we have squandered time. We have rushed so fast we missed the beauty of all that surrounds us.

Help us to live for You, and to make room for what matters most. We ask that you help us use our time wisely. Help us to delight in each day as we see You moving in the mundane and the miraculous. Teach us to set healthy limits. Encourage us to step out of our comfort zones.

Lord, we want a life with few regrets. Show us Your way – the way of abundant life and freedom.

Amen.

To Reach Me:

If you would like to read more, join me at
https://pattyhscott.com.
Resources to accompany this book are at
https://pattyhscott/slowdownmama/

You can ask me to come speak to your church,
MOPS group or other event by contacting me
through
**https://www.womenspeakers.com/bakersfield/
speaker/patty-scott**

I usually answer email within 48 hours at
pjpsalm103@sbcglobal.net

If you want to join a group of moms committed
to God and to loving intentionally while making
room for what matters most, feel free to join us
at **The Intentional Motherhood Community on
Facebook.**

May God richly bless you as you pursue a life
centered around what matters most.

~ Patty

DEDICATION

To Jon. You are the best brake pedal God could have given me. The presence of your "yes" gave me the ability to learn to say "no." Thank you for teaching me to sit still, to wait, and to be more patient. You lead by example, and I love you for your gentle strength (among many other things). Thanks for waiting for me to learn these important lessons. You are my one and only.

To my boys. I regret the moments I hurried you. I missed some precious times because of my frantic lifestyle. I let stress pour into my motherhood. Thank you for giving me second chances, and for all the joy and adventure you bring to my days. I hope the lessons in this book have been embraced and modeled by me so that you can live lives that savor the moments and make room for what matters most.

To my dear friends, mastermind group, prayer partners, and the launch team who have cheered me on as a writer and a person. You know who you are. I can't imagine this journey without your encouragement and wisdom. You have spoken truth into vulnerable places, making me see the need to change and grow. Your love has provided the safety I needed to take risks. I can't adequately find words to express my gratitude for you.

A special thanks to Dawn Benson-Jones for the hours spent refining this work with your heart for moms and your eye for details. You are a gift to me.

To the people who have blessed me through their writing about time and life. You don't even know your impact. This book is a reflection of your gifts carried forward to others. Specifically – Dan Allender, Emily P. Freeman, Greg McKeown, Crystal Paine, Lysa TerKeurst, and Alli Worthington – you are my heroes.

To God. I am in awe of Your intimate care. When I thought this book was ready to go, you unraveled me to teach me how to write more vulnerably from the heart. I am laying it all out – as You have done for me. May my words reflect even a portion of the healing goodness I have found through You. Thank you for never giving up on me. I have found rest in You and through that found the rest of me.

Cited Works

Chapter 1
1. Holz, Adam R. *Beating Busyness*. (Colorado Springs, Colorado: NavPress, 1999).

Chapter 3
1. The Holy Bible, New King James Version, Matthew 5:37. Bible Gateway. Web.
2. TerKeurst, Lysa. *The Best Yes*. (Nashville, Tennessee: Nelson Books, 2014). 59.

Chapter 4
2. Holz, Adam R. *Beating Busyness*. (Colorado Springs, Colorado: NavPress, 1999). 19.
3. The Holy Bible, New American Standard Bible Version, Psalm 23:1. Bible Gateway. Web.

Chapter 6
1. Brown, Brené. *The Power of Vulnerability*. Narrated by Brené Brown, Audible, 2012. Audiobook.
2. Stafford, Rachel Macy. *Hands Free Life*. (Grand Rapids, Michigan: Zondervan, 2015).
3. Spurgeon, Charles Haddon. All of Grace. (Lindenhurst, New York: Great Christian Books, 2012). 43.
4. Freeman, Emily P. *A Million Little Ways: Uncover the Art You Were Made to Live*. (Ada, Michigan: Revell, 2013). 24.

Chapter 7
1. Oxenrider, Tsh. *Organized Simplicity: The Clutter-Free Approach to Intentional Living*. (New York, New York: Betterway Home, 2010).

Chapter 7
2. http://www.thirteenvirtues.com/
3. The Holy Bible, New International Version, Philippians 4:5. Bible Gateway. Web.

Chapter 8
1. Allender, Dan B. *To Be Told.* (Colorado Springs, Colorado: Waterbrook, 2005). 13.
2. http://westminsterconfession.org/confessional-standards/the-westminster-shorter-catechism.php
3. McKeown, Greg. *Essentialism.* Narrated by Greg McKeown, Audible, 2014. Audiobook.

Chapter 11
1. http://www.hawaii.edu/behavior/306/downloads/Multitasking%20-%20Dzubak.pdf
2. https://www.psychologytoday.com/us/blog/the-athletes-way/201112/the-neuroscience-perseverance

Chapter 12
1. https://www.mayoclinic.org/healthy-lifestyle/stress-management/in-depth/stress-symptoms/art-20050987
2. The Holy Bible, New American Standard Bible, James 1:2. Bible Gateway. Web.
3. *Strictly Ballroom.* Dir. Baz Luhrmann. Perf. Paul Mercurio, Tara Morice, Bill Hunter. M & A, Australian Film Finance Corporation (AFFC), 1993. Motion Picture.
4. The Holy Bible, New International Version, Matthew 6: 25-34. Bible Gateway. Web.

Chapter 13
1. Worthington, Alli. *Breaking Busy: How to Find Peace and Purpose in a World of Crazy.* Narrated by Jamie Paul, Audible, 2016. Audiobook
2. Ibid.

Chapter 15
1. Worthington, Alli. *Breaking Busy: How to Find Peace and Purpose in a World of Crazy.* Narrated by Jamie Paul, Audible, 2016. Audiobook

Chapter 16
1. The Holy Bible, New International Version, Hebrews 4: 9-11. Bible Gateway. Web.
2. The Holy Bible, New International Version, 1 Thessalonians 4: 11. Bible Gateway. Web.
3. https://gospelinlife.com/downloads/work-and-rest-5314/
4. The Holy Bible, New American Standard Bible, Matthew, 11: 28. Bible Gateway. Web.

Chapter 17
1. *The Next Right Thing.* Episode 40: *Keep Your Rest.* Emily P. Freeman. Podcast.

Chapter 18
1. The Holy Bible, New International Version, Colossians 3:1-2. Bible Gateway. Web.
2. The Holy Bible, New International Version, Psalm, 46:10. Bible Gateway. Web.

Chapter 19
1. The Holy Bible, The Message Version, Colossians 3: 3-4. Bible Gateway. Web.

Chapter 19

2. Hippo, St. Augustine of. *The Confessions of St. Augustine.* Narrated by Emily Hanna, Audible, 2016. Audiobook

Chapter 21

1. McKeown, Greg. *Essentialism.* Narrated by Greg McKeown, Audible, 2014. Audiobook.
2. ibid.
3. The Holy Bible, New International Version, Proverbs, 19:21. Bible Gateway. Web.
4. The Holy Bible, New International Version, Proverbs, 16:3. Bible Gateway. Web.

Chapter 22

1. The Holy Bible, New International Version, Exodus 14: 14. Bible Gateway. Web.
2. The Holy Bible, New American Standard Bible, Matthew, 6:34. Bible Gateway. Web.
3. The Holy Bible, New American Standard, Psalms, 139:1-6. Bible Gateway. Web.
4. The Holy Bible, New International Version, Psalms, 119:105. Bible Gateway. Web.

Chapter 23

1. The Holy Bible, New International Version, Matthew 6:34. Bible Gateway. Web.

Chapter 24

1. *The Next Right Thing.* Episode 2: *Do This Before Every Hard Decision.* Emily P. Freeman. Podcast.

Chapter 25

1. McKeown, Greg. *Essentialism.* Narrated by Greg McKeown, Audible, 2014. Audiobook.

Chapter 25
2. ibid.
3. Worthington, Alli. *Breaking Busy: How to Find Peace and Purpose in a World of Crazy..* Narrated by Jamie Paul, Audible, 2016. Audiobook
4. TerKeurst, Lysa. *The Best Yes.* Narrated by Amber Quick, Audible, 2014. Audiobook.
5. Scott, Patty. Parenting Your Teen Through Chaos and Crisis. (Amazon, 2018). 83. Number
6. https://www.positivediscipline.com/articles/decide-what-you-will-do/
7. The Holy Bible. New American Standard Bible, Proverbs 15: 22. Bible Gateway. Web.

Chapter 26
1. http://news.mit.edu/2012/understanding-how-brains-control-our-habits-1029
2. Lewis, C.S. *Mere Christianity.* (New York, New York: Macmillan, 1977). 86-87.
3. https://francescocirillo.com/pages/pomodoro-technique
4. McKeown, Greg. *Essentialism.* Narrated by Greg McKeown, Audible, 2014. Audiobook.

Chapter 27
1. Scott, S.J. *Habit Stacking.* Narrated by Greg Sarcone, Audible, 2017. Audiobook.
2. https://www.youtube.com/watch?v=pxBQLFLei70
3. Bogel, Anne. https://modernmrsdarcy.com/
4. https://www.sharecare.com/health/labor-stages/transition-phase-of-labor

Chapter 28

1. Mason, Moya K.. "Housing: Then, Now, and Future." MKM Research. http://www.moyak.com/papers/house-sizes.html
2. https://www.forbes.com/sites/trulia/2017/01/24/average-price-average-size-not-your-average-home/#2a59b1dd49a1
3. McKeown, Greg. *Essentialism.* Narrated by Greg McKeown, Audible, 2014. Audiobook.

Chapter 29

1. The Holy Bible, New International Version, John 15: 5. Bible Gateway. Web.

Chapter 31

1. The Holy Bible, New American Standard Bible, Psalm 118: 24. Bible Gateway. Web.

Made in the USA
San Bernardino, CA
02 October 2018